Speech + Dra

Marywood

THE WAY OF THE MAKERS

BY
MARGUERITE WILKINSON

BLUESTONE
NEW VOICES
CONTEMPORARY POETRY
THE DINGBAT OF ARCADY
THE GREAT DREAM

THE WAY OF THE MAKERS

BY

MARGUERITE WILKINSON

Ogden (Bigelow)

New York

THE MACMILLAN COMPANY

1925

TO

MARY FRANCIS BIGELOW

KINSWOMAN AND FRIEND

ODE

We are the music-makers,
  And we are the dreamers of dreams,
Wandering by lone sea-breakers,
  And sitting by desolate streams;
World-losers and world-forsakers,
  On whom the pale moon gleams:
Yet we are the movers and shakers
  Of the world for ever, it seems.

With wonderful deathless ditties
We build up the world's great cities,
  And out of a fabulous story
  We fashion an empire's glory:
One man with a dream, at pleasure,
  Shall go forth and conquer a crown;
And three with a new song's measure
  Can trample an empire down.

We, in the ages lying
  In the buried past of the earth,
Built Nineveh with our sighing,
  And Babel itself with our mirth;
And o'erthrew them with prophesying
  To the old of the new world's worth;
For each age is a dream that is dying,
  Or one that is coming to birth.

                              —*Arthur O'Shaughnessy*

ACKNOWLEDGMENTS

The thanks of the author are due to the following publishers for their courteous permission to reprint material published under their imprint:

To The Macmillan Company for selections from "The Candle of Vision" and "Collected Poems," by A. E. (George Russell); for selections from "Letters" of Matthew Arnold; for a sonnet from "Cloister," by Charles L. O'Donnell, C.S.C.; for lyrics from "Bluestone," by Marguerite Wilkinson; for brief passages of prose by Sara Teasdale, William Rose Benét, Padraic Colum, Robert Frost, Harriet Monroe, and Edwin Markham, reprinted from "New Voices," by Marguerite Wilkinson; for "Petit, The Poet," from "The Spoon River Anthology," by Edgar Lee Masters; for selections from Mark Pattison's "Life of Milton," and Hiram Corson's "Introduction to the Works of Milton"; for passages from "Letters of Elizabeth Barrett Browning" (ed. by Kenyon); for several pages from "Memoirs of Tennyson," by Hallam Tennyson, his son; for selections from the "Prose Essays," of William Butler Yeats.

(The poetry of standard poets used in this book is taken, as a rule, from the Globe Series of poets, in which series may be found Arnold, Browning, Chaucer, Spenser, Shakespeare, Keats, Shelley, Coleridge, Wordsworth, Cowper, Tennyson, Dryden and others.)

To Messrs. Charles Scribners Sons for excerpts from "Letters of George Meredith"; for a passage from "Interpretations of Poetry and Religion," by George Santayana, and for another passage from the preface to his "Poems"; for sixteen lines from "The Crystal," by Sidney Lanier; for "The Dear Mystery" from "The Black Panther," by John Hall Wheelock; for one paragraph from "Essays and Studies" of Algernon Charles Swinburne; for a quotation from "Family Letters of Christina Rossetti," and for a number of letters from "The Letters of William Blake," and for one paragraph from Francis Thompson's "Essay on Shelley."

To Messrs. Harcourt, Brace & Co. for a page from "Poetic Madness" and two paragraphs from "Inspiration" from "The Torch and Other Lectures," by George E. Woodberry, copyright, 1920, by Harcourt, Brace and Company, Inc.; for a long passage from "Rupert Brooke and the Intellectual Imagination," by Walter de la Mare; and for selections from the letters of Shelley.

To Messrs. Houghton-Mifflin & Co. for several paragraphs from the essay called "The Poet," and for two poems, "The Poet" and "The Test," and for one sentence from "Inspiration," and for eleven lines from "Saadi," by Ralph Waldo Emerson; and for seven passages from "The Letters of Samuel Taylor Coleridge."

To Messrs. Dodd, Mead & Co. for part of the "Ballad In Blank Verse" from "Ballads and Songs," by John Davidson; for "A Poet's Prayer," by Stephen Phillips; for certain passages from the "Letters of Algernon Charles Swinburne."

To Alfred A. Knopf, Inc., for two paragraphs from "On English Poetry," by Robert Graves; for several paragraphs from "Colors of Life," by Max Eastman; for the brief introductory lyric from "Ship's Log," by Grace Hazard Conkling, and for two paragraphs from "Scepticism," by Conrad Aiken.

To Mr. George Haven Putnam, Publisher, for "The Myth of Arthur" from "The Ballad of Saint Barbara," by G. K. Chesterton; for two paragraphs from "Studies in Poetry," by Stopford Brooke; and for two lines from one of David Morton's sonnets.

To Messrs. E. P. Dutton & Co. for "The Poet and His Muse" from "The Complete Poetical Works" of James Thomson ("B.V.").

To Messrs. Henry Holt & Co. for "Hapless," from the "Collected Poems" of Walter de la Mare.

To Mr. Robert McBride for one page from "Psychology and Morals," by J. A. Hadfield.

To The George H. Doran Co. for "The Harp" from "Vigils," by Aline Kilmer.

To Messrs. Little, Brown & Co. for "A Book," by Emily Dickinson.

To Messrs. Doubleday, Page & Co. for selections from "Leaves of Grass," by Walt Whitman.

To Messrs. Longmans Green & Co. for one paragraph from "News From Nowhere," by William Morris.

To Messrs. Boni & Liveright for one page from "Troubadour," by Alfred Kreymborg.

To The Columbia University Press for several paragraphs from "Sir Walter Scott as a Critic of Literature," by Margaret Ball.

To The Oxford University Press for three paragraps from "The Necessity of Poetry," by Robert Bridges, and for several pages from their edition of "William Blake," edited by John Sampson.

To The Yale University Press for an "Ode," by Arthur O'Shaughnessy.

To Frederick A. Stokes Co. for "Paraclete," by Alfred Noyes.

To Brandt & Brandt for two paragraphs from "On English Poetry," by Robert Graves.

To *The World To-Morrow* for "A Conversation," by Babette Deutsch.

To *The New Republic* for "Jewelled Bindings," by Elinor Wylie.

And to the following poets for original contributions to this volume:

To Katharine Lee Bates for the article "Concerning Chaucer."

To Jeannette Marks for the selection from her "Disaster and Poetry."

To Anna Hempstead Branch for her comment on inspiration.

To John Masefield for his thought of poise in art.

To Amy Lowell for her article on "The Process of Making Poetry."

To John Gould Fletcher for his "Thoughts on the Making of Poetry."

To Margaret Widdemer for one paragraph on technique.

To Constance Lindsay Skinner for one paragraph on rhythm.

My thanks are also due to Caroline Singleton for her assistance in the work of research preparatory to the making of this book.

It is a matter of great regret to me that I am unable to include anything by Edna St. Vincent Millay.

MARGUERITE WILKINSON.

FOREWORD

The roots of the tree of life are all interwoven and the branches all spring from one trunk. From the deepest fiber to the loftiest twig one sap of life rises urgently. It nourishes power for reproduction and skill for labor. It creates art, science, poetry and religion. Of it may come lust or love, tyrannous activity or creative wonder, for it all depends on the way the sap is used. Lust and drudgery are ways of bondage. Joyful labor, love, poetry and religion are ways of freedom. If we are willing to use this energizing sap in the ways of bondage, life will be a dry and dusty thing in the end; but if we try, even a little, to use it in the ways of better omen, we may find our spirits growing and blossoming for an everlasting life.

The great way of liberation which I have chosen to discuss in this book is the way of the makers, the poets. It is beset with dangers. But it is a way of adventure alike for those who take it as their very own and for those who follow them sympathetically. I realize that I should not have chosen to write about it myself. I should have delegated the task to a great psychologist who could explain with conscientious elaboration many of the things which stir and fascinate me, or to an earnest critic who would avoid all the perils of receptive simplicity that he might discuss with fastidious scepticism the plaintive and peculiar accounts that poets give of their dreams, their efforts, and their achievements. Yet the task has tempted me and I have yielded to the temptation.

Therefore, be it known at the outset that I wish to be modest and unpretentious, to let the poets speak for themselves. I shall let them say what they think of their own travail and exultation. I shall merely preside at the experience meeting. And if I am arbitrary in the matter of selection, it will be because I am finite and must follow the direction that my own mind chooses to take. This is a serious limitation, but I do not know how it can be overcome.

I have found much material for study, innumerable letters, memoirs, prefaces, and other prose writings as well as poems. I have tried to choose for reproduction here such excerpts as seemed to be most pertinent, flavorous and illuminating. The reader should not judge any poet's life and thought by these excerpts alone, however, for letters and memoirs, like lyrics, often represent moods that may be fleeting. Many of the poems chosen for inclusion are used not because of their value as poetry, though many of them are excellent poems, but because they throw light on the matters under discussion.

I have tried to make this book a record of experience rather than a symposium of theories. I think poets are more interesting when they tell what has happened to them, or in them, than when they dogmatize about what ought to happen. And only poets are called to give an account of themselves in this book. Seanchan is invited to the royal table, but critics may cool their heels on the threshold.

Readers who are interested in the creative processes described in this book will be glad to know of a number of new books on the same themes. "The Poetic Mind," by Frederick Clarke Prescott; "On English Poetry," by Robert Graves; "William Blake," by S. Foster Damon, and Miss Lowell's new book on Keats will all be of interest to such readers. Also I understand that Mary Austin's new book on genius is nearly ready.

I have traversed the royal road of English poetry from Edmund Spenser to John Masefield and the broad highway of American song from Ralph Waldo Emerson to Vachel Lindsay. I have made this record for Americans who need these poets now and need to understand them better. My book is not made for scholars, but for men, women, and children who may wish to know more about their poets— how they feel, think, live, and labor. I have made it for the young students of poetry who would like to discriminate between the great and the brilliant, between the sublime and the specious. That the roots of the tree of life may strike deeper into the soil of my country, that the sap may rise higher for us, that the bloom be sweeter, may this book bring them nearer to the minds of the masters and show them the high freedom of the way of the makers. As Carl Sandburg nobly says, "The peace of great books be for you."

CONTENTS

CONTENTS

CONTENTS

ANOTHER

Yes, every poet is a fool:
  By demonstration Ned can show it;
Happy, could Ned's inverted rule
  Prove every fool to be a poet.

—Matthew Prior

THE POETIC NATURE

We all know an ancient classic of the nursery which asks what little girls are made of and answers with the names of various delectables, and then asks what little boys are made of and answers with the names of numerous comic disagreeables. If, in a similar vein, we ask what poets are made of, we shall have to admit that the delectable and the disagreeable are mingled in them, and that many things not attributed to little boys and girls are combined in their natures. Spiritually, the poet is "man and woman and child all three," having the passion of the world's manhood, the intuition and sensitivity of womanhood, and the child's overwhelming zest for life and joy in play.

Passion is truly "the sign of the poet" because, as George Edward Woodberry wisely says, "he enters into life more than other men." It is truer, perhaps, to say that life enters into him more fully than it enters into others. His senses are not narrow paths, but broad highways whereon march armies of impressions, thronging in to the citadel of his mind. That citadel is inwardly labyrinthine. It has underground passages. They are dark and filled with treasure and information, like the catacombs. Exploration is possible, though difficult and dangerous. And beneath the labyrinthine catacombs the nether floor of the citadel sometimes ebbs and shifts like a rocking ocean, or breaks open as the ground breaks with an earthquake, because emotions more profound than thought would rise as fountains or as fire. The armies of sensations and impressions throng in upon the heaving and uncertain floor. They scale the high walls of thought and engage in battles—sometimes sham fights in which the combatants are masked and mirthful, sometimes hideous or magnificent maneuvers, attacks against the walls of Paradise and defenses of Hell. Perhaps the fighters sink down into limbo at last, or drift aimlessly away when the surface of the mind is quiet, or fade out as ghosts before the sun, leaving languor and hesitation behind them. There may be a time of quietness before the next army comes in with banners flying. But something is always happening in the catacombs and below. And only the central ego of the poet in the hidden room at the center of the citadel keeps watch forever over all that is his, loving the entering armies and those that disappear in the labyrinthine alleys, and the tall, triumphant walls that shut out the world, and the heaving surface on which he rests, loving all these not only for what they are, but for what they mean, for what he can do with them.

The power of sensations and impressions in the mind of the poet must be multiplied by their numberless associations which he is able to make more quickly than others· make them. People often say that they "see red" or "feel green." The poet can taste blue and hear yellow, and that with ludicrous vividness. He can touch light and hear moisture and see flavors proclaim themselves. For him it is no untruth to say that "the dawn comes up like thunder." And if this be true of sense impressions, what shall we say of the things that transcend the senses? If you have a friend who is a poet, and if you do not wish him to know what you are thinking, do not think too loud when you are with him, lest he overhear your thought as you might hear his words! Poets, assuredly, tingle to the finger tips with feelings that do not move most people at all. And the things that do move them, the universal joys and sorrows, shake poets to the depths of their souls and are insuperable—until they have been made into poetry. Life enters into the poet so fully and so vividly that he dares not hold it all in silence. He must give it back to the world in words. As Blake says, "Joys impregnate, sorrows bring forth."

The fine frenzy and the high feigning of the poet are not merely natural to him, they are necessary. And yet, though that may be true on the human side, it is not enough to say. For the artist, the central ego, finds the deepest peace and the highest exultation in using for mankind the materials of his travail, in forming into images of life the experience that could not otherwise be borne. That is why the thwarted poet becomes gloomy and morbid. That is why the poet whose necessary labor for a living balks his expression becomes irritable. He cannot afford what Chatterton calls "the wild expenses of a poet's brain."

There is an equilibrium, then, or there should be, between the throes of passion in the poet and his power to utilize passion in creation. The greatest of all the masters have learned that equilibrium. Coleridge says that Shakespeare's evenness and sweetness of temper were almost proverbial in his own age, that in Spenser we nowhere find "the least trace of irritability, and still less of quarrelsome or affected contempt of his censurers" and that "the same

calmness and even greater self-possession may be affirmed
of Milton, as far as his poems and his poetic character are
concerned." These were men of the greatest genius who
achieved fullest expression. John Masefield is right when
he says that art demands a balance or steadiness of nature,
and that, although much beautiful art has been given to
the world by men suffering from disease of one sort or
another, the best art is the result of superb health of mind
and body. But let us be gentle with the lesser geniuses who
have not achieved this serene poise. We may judge of the
difficulty of achieving it by the rarity of the genius that
does. All true genius, as the earlier James Thomson says,
would be always "beaming forth". Let us be thankful
even for the intermittent lights.

As for the discrepancy that sometimes exists between
the morals of poets and the radiance of their vision, it were
well for the stolid, practical person to be charitable. Without condoning serious flaws in character, without taking the
sort of noxious pleasure in them that enjoys sin, as it were,
by proxy, let him remember that the poet is not necessarily
of a fiber weaker than his own, but is much more sensi-
tively attuned to life and more likely to be beset by eco-
nomic difficulties, and therefore may be more furiously
tempted. Says Herrick, that jaunty clergyman of "the
tribe of Ben" who made Julia immortal and let his pet pig
drink from his own tankard,

> Wantons we are; and though our words be such,
> Our lives do differ from our lines by much.

But certainly I ought not to ask any license for poets.
Wrong is wrong even if a poet does it. The world is often

too indulgent with them. The world likes to believe that they are foolish, irresponsible, romantic creatures—not merely sinners like other people. As Max Eastman has wittily said in *The Enjoyment of Poetry,* "It appears that a poet in history is divine, but a poet in the next room is a joke." So be it. The last laugh is best. A poet is not the lofty creature, finely polished and ready for heavenly society that he often seems to be to the class of adolescents in high school who study his work and incline toward hero worship. But, on the other hand, the public of to-day pays its poets a spurious compliment when it condones in them behavior that it would condemn in others, when it allows and encourages the absurd belief that poets must drink a mean draught of evil and make wry faces over it before they can pour out the pure wine of life. Milton tells the truth when he says that the man who would write of gods and heroes and high affairs should have rigid morals and hands free from stain. The dignity of the art demands dignity of the artist.

When poets are irresponsible it is often because they are childlike, the fault being a correlative of a virtue essential to art. The poet keeps always something of the verve, the naturalness and the spontaneity of childhood. When he is joyful his joy is "unconfined." When he is sorrowful he breaks his heart on the breast of his mother the earth. When he makes his poems he is, as Thompson said of Shelley, "still at play, save only that his play is such as manhood stops to watch, and his playthings are those which the gods give their children." The later James Thompson called Blake "the giant who became a child." Emerson said of any poet,

> A moody child and wildly wise
> Pursued the game with joyful eyes.

And Coleridge said that he felt like a child in the presence of certain of his contemporaries.

Poets all know how he felt. They know because they themselves are often helpless in the company of busy, prosperous, worldly-wise people. Something that is native and appropriate to the poet as an atmosphere is missing and he fades out and loses himself for the nonce. He grows dumb and numb and awkward to the point of fright. Nevertheless it is not crudity or vulgarity that alarms him, for, as Coleridge says somewhat too snobbishly, "men of genius rarely are much annoyed by the company of vulgar people, because they have a power of looking *at* such persons as objects of amusement of another race altogether," and it is well known that in a much finer spirit many living poets prefer the society of peasants to the society of ordinary intellectuals as being a shorter cut to reality of experience, and, perhaps, an opportunity for quicker and keener sympathy. People may be as crude as they like, as vulgar as they like, or even as prosperous as they like with a poet provided only that they have a real and warm sympathy to offer him which is of a kind that he desires. A poet can be quite happy at a hobo's bonfire if the talk is entertaining and the general tone of the gathering informal and friendly. If your poet is really shy and unconventional, not merely affected, pity his helplessness, for it is *sancta simplicitas!* To quote Coleridge once more: "Can mere juxtaposition form a neighborhood? As well should the louse in my head call himself my friend, and the flea in my bosom style herself my love!''

If poets seem graceless and unaccountable in their whims about people, it is due them to observe that their real friendships are often sincere, strong and lasting. Many of the masters of English song have been both fine and fortunate in their boon comrades. This may be because they are chosen for sympathy, not for convenience. There is nothing arbitrary in such associations save the laws of nature that made them seem desirable to those concerned. Yet dear as the sympathy of friends is to poets, and some of them seem to live by it, they are always just leaving it for solitude unless they are leaving solitude for sympathy. It is of the nature of poets to live always more or less in contrasted experiences.

Probably this is because contrasts and alternations heighten the emotional effects of life's events. Intense creative activity is followed by languor and it is the meadow longest fallow that should be sown for song. How hard that fate, for the sake of producing what the race sorely needs and is slow to accept, must curse human creatures with such fiery and conflicting desires! Therein is the source of their ''wild wisdom.''

It is the wisdom of the mind that knows itself well, that has probed deep wounds and touched high glories. It is a wisdom that comes from the individual subconsciousness where truth reigns supreme and from the greater contiguous subconsciousness of the world and from the racial memory. It is a wisdom quickened and stimulated by emotion, not formulated by rational processes working alone.

It is the fruit of inspiration and the seed of prophecy. It is never prudential. It is often incalculable. It is always ineffaceable.

So much for the intoxication of the genius and the use of it in poetry. It is necessary to say that there is a counterfeit. There is a poet, so-called, whose desire to write sensationally leads him out in quest of excitement. Since clean, strong, true ecstasy seldom pursues him, he goes on bush-whacking expeditions and finds brain storms. When he has converted the spurious substitute into extravagant words and given it a novel title and secured exploitation for it, he is content. *Requiescat in pace!* The world will not long mistake rage for inspiration.

One poet differs from another in glory, to be sure, and in other ways,—in appetite, health, manner, and ambition. Yet in a few things one poet is much like another. Worlds that are unreal to others are real to poets and worlds that are real to others are unreal to them. They are sometimes absent-minded on earth to be present-minded in fairyland, and conversely, they are sometimes absent-minded in an earthly Paradise to be present-minded in a shoe factory. They are capable of innumerable quaintnesses and quiddities. Nobody but a poet could be as pompous as Wordsworth is about the terrier mentioned in "The Prelude"! They are prone to exaggeration and vehemence. They will dream by night if they cannot dream by day, or by day if they may not dream by night. They will call tempests out of clear heavens and speak peace to stormy hours. They will be rash and free. Yet it by no means follows that they are always impractical. Barry Cornwall's wife wrote to Tennyson's son, saying,

I have known three great poets, Wordsworth, Browning, and your father, and when they chose they could be more prosaic and practical than anybody on earth.

But though he may be practical in connection with the practical side of life, one thing the valid poet always hates —any lowering of the standard of art for the sake of quick and easy success. Though he starve for it, he will be himself. As Ben Jonson said,

> Though need make many poets, and some such
> As art and nature have not bettered much;
> Yet ours for want hath not so loved the stage
> As he dare serve the ill customs of an age,
> Or purchase your delight at such a rate,
> As, for it, he himself must justly hate.

From "A Midsummer Night's Dream."
Lovers and madmen have such seething brains,
Such shaping fantasies, that apprehend
More than cool reason ever comprehends.
The lunatic, the lover and the poet
Are of imagination all compact:
One sees more devils than vast hell can hold,
That is, the madman: the lover, all as frantic,
Sees Helen's beauty in a brow of Egypt:
The poet's eye, in a fine frenzy rolling,
Doth glance from heaven to earth, from earth to heaven;
And as imagination bodies forth

The forms of things unknown, the poet's pen
Turns them to shapes and gives to airy nothing
A local habitation and a name.
Such tricks hath strong imagination,
That, if it would but apprehend some joy,
It comprehends some bringer of that joy;
Or in the night, imagining some fear,
How easy is a bush supposed a bear!

—*William Shakespeare*

From "As You Like It."

SCENE III. *The forest.*

Enter TOUCHSTONE *and* AUDREY; JAQUES *behind.*

Touch. Come apace, good Audrey: I will fetch up your goats, Audrey. And how, Audrey? am I the man yet? doth my simple feature content you?

Aud. Your features! Lord warrant us! what features?

Touch. I am here with thee and thy goats, as the most capricious poet, honest Ovid, was among the Goths.

Jaq. (*Aside*) O knowledge ill-inhabited, worse than Jove in a thatched house!

Touch. When a man's verses cannot be understood, nor a man's good wit seconded with the forward child Understanding, it strikes a man more dead than a great reckoning in a little room. Truly, I would the gods had made thee poetical.

Aud. I do not know what "poetical" is: is it honest in deed and word? is it a true thing?

Touch. No, truly; for the truest poetry is the most

feigning; and lovers are given to poetry, and what they swear in poetry may be said as lovers they do feign.

Aud. Do you wish then that the gods had made me poetical?

Touch. I do, truly; for thou swearest to me thou art honest: now, if thou wert a poet, I might have some hope thou didst feign.

Aud. Would you not have me honest?

Touch. No, truly, unless thou wert hard-favoured; for honesty coupled to beauty is to have honey a sauce to sugar.

Jaq. (*Aside*) A material fool!

Aud. Well, I am not fair; and therefore I pray the gods make me honest.

—*William Shakespeare*

From "Poetic Madness."

The sign of the poet, then, is that by passion he enters into life more than other men. That is his gift—the power to live. The lives of poets are but little known; but from the fragments of their lives that come down to us, the characteristic legend is that they have been singularly creatures of passion. They lived before they sang. Emotion is the condition of their existence; passion is the element of their being; and, moreover, the intensifying power of such a state of passion must also be remembered, for emotion of itself naturally heightens all the faculties, and genius burns the brighter in its own flames. The poet craves emotion, and feeds the fire that consumes him, and only under this condition is he baptized with creative power. It is to be expected, therefore, that the tradition of the poet's life should have an element of strangeness in it; and, in fact, to neglect those cases where genius has touched the border of actual madness, every poet has this stamp of destiny set upon him. There is always some wildness in his nature; he is apt to be roving, adventurous, unforeseen; he is without fear, he is careless of his life; he is not to be commanded; freedom is what he most dearly loves, and he will have it at any peril; that from which he will not be divided is the primeval heritage, the Dionysiac madness that resides not only in the instincts, but in all the faculties of man—the power and the passion to live. It is a widespread error, and due only to the academic secondhand practice of poetry, to oppose the poet to the man of action, or assign to him a merely contemplative rôle in life, or in other ways deny reality to the poet's experience; intensity of living is preliminary to all great expression. From the beginning, about the rude altar of the god, to the days of Goethe, of Leopardi, and of Victor Hugo, the poet is the leader in the dance of life; and the phrase by which we name his singularity, the poetic temperament, denotes the primacy of that passion in his blood with which the frame of other men is less richly charged.

—*George Edward Woodberry*

From the "Essay on Shelley."

Perhaps none of his poems is more purely and typically Shelleian than *The Cloud*, and it is interesting to note how essentially it springs from the faculty of make-believe.

The same thing is conspicuous, though less purely conspicuous, throughout his singing; it is the child's faculty of make-believe raised to the nth power. He is still at play, save only that his play is such as manhood stops to watch, and his playthings are those which the gods give their children. The universe is his box of toys. He dabbles his fingers in the dayfall. He is gold-dusty with tumbling amidst the stars. He makes bright mischief with the moon. The meteors nuzzle their noses in his hand. He teases into growling the kennelled thunder, and laughs at the shaking of its fiery chain. He dances in and out of the gates of heaven; its floor is littered with his broken fancies. He runs wild over the fields of ether. He chases the rolling world. He gets between the feet of the horses of the sun. He stands in the lap of patient Nature, and twines her loosened tresses after a hundred wilful fashions, to see how she will look nicest in his song.

—Francis Thompson

THE POET

A moody child and wildly wise
Pursued the game with joyful eyes,
Which chose, like meteors, their way,
And rived the dark with private ray.
They overleaped the horizon's edge,
Searched with Apollo's privilege;
Through man, and woman, and sea, and star
Saw the dance of nature forward far;

Through worlds, and races, and terms, and times
Saw musical order and pairing rhymes.

　　　　　　　　　　　—Ralph Waldo Emerson

From "Rupert Brooke and the Intellectual Imagination."

One evening in 1766, Dr. Johnson being then in the
fifty-seventh year of his age, his friends, Boswell and
Goldsmith, called on him at his lodgings in Fleet Street.
They thereupon endeavoured in vain to persuade him to
sup with them at the Mitre. But though he was adamant
to their cajoleries, he was by no means averse to a talk.
With true hospitality, since he had himself, we are told,
become a water-drinker, he called for a bottle of port.
This his guests proceeded to discuss. While they sipped,
the three of them conversed on no less beguiling a subject
than that of play-going and poetry.

Goldsmith ventured to refer to the deplorable fact that
his old friend and former schoolfellow had given up the
writing of verses. "Why, sir," replied Johnson, "our
tastes greatly alter. The lad does not care for the child's
rattle. . . . As we advance in the journey of life, we
drop some of the things which have pleased us; whether
it be that we are fatigued and don't choose to carry so
many things any farther, or that we find other things
which we like better."

Boswell persisted. "But, sir," said he, "why don't you
give us something in some other way?" "No, sir," Johnson replied, "I am not obliged to do any more. No man
is obliged to do as much as he can do. A man is to have
part of his life to himself." "But I wonder, sir," Boswell

continued, "you have not more pleasure in writing than in not writing." Whereupon descended the crushing retort, "Sir, you *may* wonder."

Johnson then proceeded to discuss the actual making of verses. "The great difficulty," he observed—alas, how truly, "is to know when you have made good ones." Once, he boasted, he had written as many as a full hundred lines a day; but he was then under forty, and had been inspired by no less fertile a theme than "The Vanity of Human Wishes," a poem that, with other prudent counsel, bids the "young enthusiast" pause ere he choose literature and learning as a spiral staircase to fame:

> Deign on the passing world to turn thine eyes
> And pause a while for Letters to be wise. . . .

None the less, Johnson made haste to assure Goldsmith that his Muse even at this late day was not wholly mum: "I am not quite idle; I made one line t'other day; but I made no more." "Let us hear it," cried Goldsmith; "we'll put a bad one to it!" "No, sir; I have forgot it." And so sally succeeded sally.

* * * * *

"The lad does not care for the child's rattle." Here, surely, is one of those signposts, one more pressing invitation to explore. By rattle, obviously, Johnson meant not only things childish, but things childlike. For such things the "lad" does not merely cease to care. He substitutes for them other things which he likes better. Not that every vestige of charm and sentiment necessarily deserts the rattle, but other delights intrude; and, what is still more important, other faculties that will take pleasure in these new toys and interests come into energy and play. Does not this rightly imply that between childhood and boyhood is fixed a great gulf, physical, spiritual, psychological, and that in minds in which the powers and tendencies conspicuous in boyhood, and more or less dormant or latent in earlier years, predominate, those of childhood are apt to fade and fall away?

* * * * *

What are the salient characteristics of childhood? Children, it will be agreed, live in a world peculiarly their own, so much that it is doubtful if the adult can do more than very fleetingly reoccupy that faraway consciousness. There is, however, no doubt that the world of the grownup is to children an inexhaustible astonishment and despair. They brood on us. And perhaps it is well that we are not invited to their pow-wows, until, at any rate, the hatchet for the hundredth time is reburied. Children are in a sense butterflies, though they toil with an almost inconceivable assiduity after life's scanty pollen and nectar, and though, by a curious inversion of the processes of nature, they become the half-comatose and purblind crysalides which too many of us poor mature creatures so ruefully resemble. They are not bound in by their groping senses. Facts to them are the liveliest of chameleons. Between their dream and their reality looms no impassible abyss. There is no solitude more secluded than a child's, no absorption more complete, no insight more exquisite and, one might even add, more comprehensive. As we strive to look back and to live our past again, can we recall any joy, fear, hope or disappointment so extreme as those of our childhood, any love more impulsive and unquestioning, and, alas, any boredom so unmitigated and unutterable?

* * * *

We speak indulgently of childish make-believe, childish fancy. Bret Harte was nearer the truth when he maintained that "the dominant expression of a child is gravity." The cold fact is that few of us have the energy to be serious at their pitch. There runs a jingle:

> O, whither go all the nights and days?
> And where can to-morrow be?
> Is anyone there, when *I'm* not there?
> And why am I always Me?

* * * *

This broken dream, then, this profound self-communion, this innocent peace and wonder make up the secret existence of a really childlike child: while the intellect is only stirring.

Then, suddenly life flings open the door of the nursery. The child becomes a boy. I do not mean that the transformation is as instantaneous as that, though, if I may venture to give a personal testimony, I have seen two children venture out into the morning for the first time to their first boys'-school, and return at evening transmogrified, so to speak, into that queer, wild, and (frequently) amiable animal known as a boy. Gradually the childish self retires like a shocked snail into its shell. Like a hermit crab it accumulates defensive and aggressive disguises. Consciousness from being chiefly subjective becomes largely objective. The steam-engine routs Fairie. Actuality breaks in upon dream. School rounds off the glistening angles. The individual is swamped awhile by the collective. Yet the child-mind, the child-imagination, persists, and, if powerful, never perishes.

But *here,* as it seems to me, is the dividing line. It is here that the boyish type of mind and imagination, the intellectual analytical type begins to show itself, and to flourish.

*　*　*　*　*

And the poets? They, too, attend both schools. But what are the faculties and qualities of mind which produce poetry, or which incline us toward it? According to Byron, there are four elements that we are justified in demanding of a poet. He found them, not without satisfaction, more conspicuous in Pope than in his contemporaries. These elements are sense, learning (in moderation), passion and invention. Perhaps because he was less rich in it, he omitted a fifth element, by no means the least essential. I mean imagination, the imagination that not merely invents, but that creates, and pierces to the inmost spirit and being of life, humanity and nature. This poetic imagination also is of two distinct kinds or types: the one divines, the other discovers. The one is intuitive, inductive; the other logical, deductive. The one visionary, the other intellectual. The one knows that beauty is truth, the other proves that truth is beauty. And the poet inherits, as it seems to me, the one kind from the child in him, the other from the boy in him. Not that any one poet's imagination is

purely and solely of either type. The greatest poets—
Shakespeare, Dante, Goethe, for instance—are masters of
both. There is a borderland in which dwell Wordsworth,
Keats, and many others. But the visionaries, the mystics,
Plato, Plotinus, the writer of the Book of Job, Blake,
Patmore, and in our own day, Flecker, and Mr. John
Freeman, may be taken as representative of the one type;
Lucretius, Donne, Dryden, Pope, Browning, Meredith, and
in our own day, Mr. Abercrombie, may be taken as repre-
sentative of the other.

—*Walter de la Mare*

From "The Poet."

For poetry was all written before time was, and whenever we are so finely organized that we can penetrate into
that region where the air is music, we hear those primal
warblings, and attempt to write them down, but we lose
ever and anon a word, or a verse, and substitute something
of our own, and thus miswrite the poem. The men of
more delicate ear write down these cadences more faithfully, and these transcripts, though imperfect, become the
songs of the nations. For nature is as truly beautiful as
it is good, or as it is reasonable, and must as much appear,
as it must be done, or be known. Words and deeds are
quite indifferent modes of the divine energy. Words are
also actions, and actions are a kind of words.

The sign and credentials of the poet are, that he an-
nounces that which no man foretold. He is the true and
only doctor; he knows and tells; he is the only teller of

news, for he was present and privy to the appearance
which he describes. He is a beholder of ideas, and an
utterer of the necessary and casual. For we do not speak
now of men of political talents, or of industry and skill in
meter, but of the true poet. I took part in a conversation
the other day concerning a recent writer of lyrics, a man
of subtle mind, whose head appeared to be a music-box of
delicate tunes and rhythms, and whose skill, and command
of language, we could not sufficiently praise. But when
the question arose, whether he was not only a lyrist, but
a poet, we were obliged to confess that he is plainly a contemporary, not an eternal man. He does not stand out
of our low limitation, like a Chimborazo under the line,
running up from the torrid base through all the climates
of the globe, with belts of the herbage of every latitude on
its high and mottled sides; but this genius is the land-
scape-garden of a modern house, adorned with fountains
and statues, with well-bred men and women standing and
sitting in the walks and terraces. We hear, through all
the varied music, the ground-tone of conventional life.
Our poets are men of talents who sing, and not the children
of music. The argument is secondary, the finish of the
verses is primary.

For it is not meters, but a meter-making argument, that
makes a poem—a thought so passionate and alive that, like
the spirit of a plant or an animal, it has an architecture of
its own, and adorns nature with a new thing. The thought
and the form are equal in the order of time, but in the
order of genesis the thought is prior to the form. The poet
has a new thought; he has a whole new experience to
unfold; he will tell us how it was with him, and all men

will be the richer in his fortune. For the experience of each new age requires a new confession, and the world seems always waiting for its poet.

—*Ralph Waldo Emerson*

From "The Prelude."
   I was as sensitive as waters are
   To the sky's influence in a kindred mood
   Of passion; was obedient as a lute
   That waits upon the touches of the wind.
   Unknown, unthought of, yet I was most rich—
   I had a world about me—'twas my own;
   I made it, for it only lived to me,
   And to the God who sees into the heart.
   Such sympathies, though rarely, were betrayed
   By outward gestures and by visible looks:
   Some called it madness—so indeed it was,
   If child-like fruitlessness in passing joy,
   To steady moods of thoughtfulness matured
   To inspiration, sort with such a name;
   If prophecy be madness; if things viewed
   By poets in old time, and higher up
   By the first men, earth's first inhabitants,
   May in these tutored days no more be seen
   With undisordered sight. But leaving this,
   It was no madness, for the bodily eye
   Amid my strongest workings evermore
   Was searching out the lines of difference
   As they lie hid in all external forms,
   Near or remote, minute or vast; an eye

Which, from a tree, a stone, a withered leaf,
To the broad ocean and the azure heavens
Spangled with kindred multitudes of stars,
Could find no surface where its power might sleep;
Which spake perpetual logic to my soul,
And by an unrelenting agency
Did bind my feelings even as in a chain.

And here, O Friend! have I retraced my life
Up to an eminence, and told a tale
Of matters which not falsely may be called
The glory of my youth. Of genius, power,
Creation and divinity itself
I have been speaking, for my theme has been
What passed within me. Not of outward things
Done visibly for other minds, words, signs,
Symbols or actions, but of my own heart
Have I been speaking, and my youthful mind.
O Heavens! how awful is the might of souls,
And what they do within themselves while yet
The yoke of earth is new to them, the world
Nothing but a wild field where they were sown.
This is, in truth, heroic argument,
This genuine prowess, which I wished to touch
With hand however weak, but in the main
It lies far hidden from the reach of words.
Points have we all of us within our souls
Where all stand single; this I feel, and make
Breathings for incommunicable powers;
But is not each a memory to himself,

And, therefore, now that we must quit this theme,
I am not heartless, for there's not a man
That lives who hath not known his godlike hours,
And feels not what an empire we inherit
As natural beings in the strength of Nature.

Among the favourites whom it pleased me well
To see again, was one by ancient right
Our inmate, a rough terrier of the hills;
By birth and call of nature pre-ordained
To hunt the badger and unearth the fox
Among the impervious crags, but having been
From youth our own adopted, he had passed
Into a gentler service. And when first
The boyish spirit flagged, and day by day
Along my veins I kindled with the stir,
The fermentation, and the vernal heat
Of poesy, affecting private shades
Like a sick Lover, then this dog was used
To watch me, an attendant and a friend,
Obsequious to my steps early and late,
Though often of such dilatory walk
Tired, and uneasy at the halts I made.
A hundred times when, roving high and low,
I have been harassed with the toil of verse,
Much pains and little progress, and at once
Some lovely Image in the song rose up
Full-formed, like Venus rising from the sea;
Then have I darted forwards to let loose
My hand upon his back with stormy joy,

Magnificent
The morning rose, in memorable pomp,
Glorious as e'er I had beheld—in front,
The sea lay laughing at a distance; near,
The solid mountains shone, bright as the clouds,
Grain-tinctured, drenched in empyrean light;
And in the meadows and the lower grounds
Was all the sweetness of a common dawn—
Dews, vapours, and the melody of birds,
And labourers going forth to till the fields.
Ah! need I say, dear Friend! that to the brim
My heart was full; I made no vows, but vows
Were then made for me; bond unknown to me
Was given, that I should be, else sinning greatly,
A dedicated Spirit. On I walked
In thankful blessedness, which yet survives.

—William Wordsworth

From "Letters of Samuel Taylor Coleridge." To Thomas Poole.

I shall have six companions: My Sara, my babe, my own shaping and disquisitive mind, my books, my beloved friend, Thomas Poole, and lastly, Nature, looking at me with a thousand looks of beauty, and speaking to me in a thousand melodies of love. If I were capable of being tired with all these, I should then detect a vice in my nature, and would fly to habitual solitude to eradicate it.

Yes, my friend, while I opened your letter my heart was glowing with enthusiasm towards you. How little did I expect that I should find you earnestly and vehemently persuading me to prefer Acton to Stowey, and in return for the loss of your society recommending *Mr. King's* family as "very pleasant neighbours." Neighbours! Can mere juxtaposition form a neighbourhood? As well should the louse in my head call himself my friend, and the flea in my bosom style herself my love!

—*Samuel Taylor Coleridge*

From "Letters of Samuel Taylor Coleridge." To Thomas Poole.

I wrote the former letter immediately on receipt of yours, in the first flutter of agitation. The tumult of my spirits has now subsided, but the Damp struck into my very heart; and there I feel it. O my God! my God! where am I to find rest? Disappointment follows disappointment, and Hope seems given me merely to prevent my becoming callous to Misery. Now I know not where to turn myself. I was on my way to the City Library, and wrote an answer to it there. Since I have returned I have been poring into a book, as a shew for not looking at my wife and the baby. My God, I dare not look at them. Acton! The very name makes me grind my teeth! What am I to do there?

"You will have a good garden: you may, I doubt not, have ground." But am I not ignorant as a child of everything that concerns the garden and the ground? and shall I have one human being there who will instruct me? The House too—what should I do with it? We want but two rooms, or three at the furthest. And the country around is intolerably flat. I would as soon live on the banks of a Dutch canal! And no one human being near me for whom I should, or could, care a rush!

—*Samuel Taylor Coleridge*

From "Anima Poetae."

My inner mind does not justify the thought that I possess a genius, my *strength* is so very small in proportion to my power. I believe that I first, from internal feeling, made or gave light and impulse to this important distinction between strength and power, the oak and the tropic annual, or biennial, which grows nearly as high and spreads as large as the oak, but in which the *mood*, the *heart* is wanting—the vital works vehemently, but the immortal is not with it. And yet, I think, I must have some analogue of genius; because among other things, when I am in company with Mr. Sharp, Sir J. Mackintosh, R. and Sydney Smith, Mr. Scarlett, etc., etc., I feel like a child, nay, rather like an inhabitant of another planet. Their very faces all act upon me, sometimes, as if they were ghosts, but more often as if I were a ghost among them—at all times as if we were not consubstantial.

—*Samuel Taylor Coleridge*

From "Letters of Samuel Taylor Coleridge." To Thomas Poole.

. . . I remember that at eight years old I walked with him one winter evening from a farmer's house, a mile from Ottery, and he told me the names of the stars and how Jupiter was a thousand times larger than our world, and that the other twinkling stars were suns that had worlds rolling around them; and when I came home he shewed me how they rolled around. I heard him with a profound delight and admiration: but without the least mixture of wonder or incredulity. For from my early reading of fairy tales and genii, etc., etc., my mind had been habituated *to the Vast,* and I never regarded *my senses* in any way as the criteria of my belief. I regulated all my creeds by my conceptions, not by my *sight,* even at that age. Should children be permitted to read romances, and relations of giants and magicians and genii? I know all that has been said against it; but I have formed my faith in the affirmative. I know no other way of giving the mind a love of the Great and the Whole. Those who have been led to the same truths step by step, through the constant testimony of their senses, seem to me to want a sense which I possess. They contemplate nothing but *parts,* and all *parts* are necessarily little. And the universe to them is but a mass of *little things.* It is true, that the mind *may* become credulous and prone to superstition by the former method; but are not the experimentalists credulous even to madness in believing any absurdity, rather than believe the grandest truths, if they have not the testimony of their own senses in their favour?

—*Samuel Taylor Coleridge*

From "Biographia Literaria."

The poet, described in ideal perfection, brings the whole soul of man into activity, with the subordination of its faculties to each other according to their relative worth and dignity. He diffuses a tone of spirit and unity, that blends, and (as it were) *fuses*, each into each, by that synthetic and magical power, to which I would exclusively appropriate the name of Imagination. This power, first put in action by the will and understanding, and retained under their irremissive, though gentle and unnoticed, control, *laxis effertur habenis*, reveals itself in the balance or reconcilement of opposite or discordant qualities; of sameness, with difference; of the general with the concrete; the idea with the image; the individual with the representative; the sense of novelty and freshness with old and familiar objects; a more than usual state of emotion with more than usual order; judgment ever awake and steady self-possession with enthusiasm and feeling profound or vehement; and while it blends and harmonizes the natural and the artificial, still subordinates art to nature; the manner to the matter; and our admiration of the poet to our sympathy with the poetry.

*　　*　　*　　*　　*　　*

The men of the greatest genius, as far as we can judge from their own works, or from the accounts of their contemporaries, appear to have been of calm and tranquil temper in all that related to themselves. In the inward assurance of permanent fame, they seem to have been either indifferent or resigned with regard to immediate reputation. Through all the works of Chaucer there reigns a cheerfulness, a manly hilarity, which makes it almost impossible to doubt a corresponding habit of feeling in the author himself. Shakespeare's evenness and sweetness of temper were almost proverbial in his own age.

—*Samuel Taylor Coleridge*

From "Memoir of James Thomson." 1700-1748.

What you observe concerning the pursuit of poetry
(so far engaged in it as I am) is certainly just. Besides,
let him quit it who can, and 'erit mihi magnus Apollo,'
or something as great. A true genius, like light, must be
beaming forth, as a false one is an incurable disease. One
would not, however, climb Parnassus, any more than your
mortal hills, to fix for ever on the barren top. No: it is
some little dear retirement in the vale below that gives the
right relish to the prospect, which, without that, is nothing
but enchantment; and though pleasing for some time, at
last leaves us in the desert. The great fat doctor of Bath
told me that poets should be kept poor, the more to ani-
mate their genius. This is like the cruel custom of putting
a bird's eye out, that it may sing the sweeter; but, surely,
they sing sweetest amidst the luxuriant woods, whilst the
full spring blooms around them.

—James Thomson

SONGS OF EXPERIENCE

Introduction

Hear the voice of the Bard!
Who present, past, and future, sees;
Whose ears have heard
The Holy Word
That walk'd among the ancient trees,

Calling the lapsèd soul,
And weeping in the evening dew;

That might control
The starry pole,
And fallen, fallen light renew!

"O Earth, O Earth, return!
Arise from out the dewy grass;
Night is worn,
And the morn
Rises from the slumberous mass.

"Turn away no more;
Why wilt thou turn away.
The starry floor,
The wat'ry shore,
Is giv'n thee till the break of day."

—*William Blake*

From "Prometheus Unbound."
On a poet's lips I slept
Dreaming like a love-adept
In the sound his breathing kept;
Nor seeks nor finds he mortal blisses,
But feeds on the aërial kisses
Of shapes that haunt thought's wildernesses.
He will watch from dawn to gloom
The lake-reflected sun illume
The yellow bees in the ivy-bloom,
Nor heed nor see, what things they be;
But from these create he can
Forms more real than living man,

Nurslings of immortality!
One of these awakened me,
And I sped to succour thee.

Percy Bysshe Shelley

From the preface to "Alastor."

The poem entitled *Alastor* may be considered as allegorical of one of the most interesting situations of the
human mind. It represents a youth of uncorrupted feelings and adventurous genius led forth by an imagination
inflamed and purified through familiarity with all that is
excellent and majestic, to the contemplation of the universe. He drinks deep of the fountains of knowledge, and
is still insatiate. The magnificence and beauty of the external world sinks profoundly into the frame of his conceptions, and affords to their modifications, a variety not
to be exhausted. So long as it is possible for his desires
to point towards objects thus infinite and unmeasured, he
is joyous, and tranquil, and self-possessed. But the period
arrives when these objects cease to suffice. His mind is at
length suddenly awakened and thirsts for intercourse with
an intelligence similar to itself. He images to himself
the Being whom he loves. Conversant with speculations
of the sublimest and most perfect natures, the vision in
which he embodies his own imaginations unites all of wonderful, or wise, or beautiful, which the poet, the philosopher, or the lover could depicture. The intellectual
faculties, the imagination, the functions of sense, have
their respective requisitions on the sympathy of corresponding powers in other human beings. The Poet is

represented as uniting these requisitions, and attaching them to a single image. He seeks in vain for a prototype of his conception. Blasted by his disappointment, he descends to an untimely grave.

The picture is not barren of instruction to actual men. The Poet's self-centred seclusion was avenged by the furies of an irresistible passion pursuing him to speedy ruin. But that Power which strikes the luminaries of the world with sudden darkness and extinction, by awakening them to too exquisite a perception of its influences, dooms to a slow and poisonous decay those meaner spirits that dare to abjure its dominion. Their destiny is more abject and inglorious as their delinquency is more contemptible and pernicious. They who, deluded by no generous error, instigated by no sacred thirst of doubtful knowledge, duped by no illustrious superstition, loving nothing on this earth, and cherishing no hopes beyond, yet keep aloof from sympathies with their kind, rejoicing neither in human joy nor mourning with human grief; these, and such as they, have their apportioned curse. They languish, because none feel with them their common nature. They are morally dead. They are neither friends, nor lovers, nor fathers, nor citizens of the world, nor benefactors of their country. Among those who attempt to exist without human sympathy, the pure and tender-hearted perish through the intensity and passion of their search after its communities, when the vacancy of their spirit suddenly makes itself felt. All else, selfish, blind, and torpid, are those unforeseeing multitudes who constitute together with their own, the lasting misery and loneliness of the world. Those who love not their fellow-beings live unfruitful lives, and prepare for their old age a miserable grave.

"The good die first,
And those whose hearts are dry as summer dust,
Burn to the socket!"

—*Percy Bysshe Shelley*

From "Letters of Percy Bysshe Shelley," to Mary Wollstonecraft Shelley.

My greatest content would be to desert all human society. I would retire with you and our child to a solitary island in the sea, would build a boat, and shut upon my retreat the floodgates of the world. I should read no reviews, and talk with no authors. If I dared trust my imagination, it would tell me that there are one or two chosen companions besides yourself whom I should desire. But to this I would not listen—where two or three are gathered together, the devil is among them. And good, far more than evil impulses, love, far more than hatred, has been to me, except as you have been its object, the source of all sorts of mischief. So on this plan, I would be *alone,* and would devote, either to oblivion or to future generations, the overflowings of a mind which, timely withdrawn from the contagion, should be kept fit for no baser object. But this it does not appear we shall do.

—*Percy Bysshe Shelley*

From "Letters and Journals of Byron," by Moore.

I do not know that I am happiest when alone; but this I am sure of, that I never am long in the society even of *her* I love (God knows too well, and the Devil probably too), without a yearning for the company of my lamp and my utterly confused and tumbled-over library. Even in the day, I send away my carriage oftener than I use or abuse it. *Per esempio,*—I have not stirred out of these rooms for these four days past: but I have sparred for exercise (windows open) with Jackson an hour daily, to attenuate and keep up the ethereal part of me. The more violent the fatigue, the better my spirits for the rest of the day; and then, my evenings have that calm nothingness of languor, which I most delight in. To-day I have boxed one hour—written an ode to Napoleon Buonaparte —copied it—eaten six biscuits—drunk four bottles of soda water—redde away the rest of my time—besides giving poor —— a world of advice about this mistress of his, who is plaguing him into a phthisic and intolerable tediousness.

—*Lord Byron*

From "The Letters of Algernon Charles Swinburne," Gosse and Wise. To Edmund Clarence Stedman.

So much for family history; which may be a stupid matter, but to write about my personality is to me yet more so. My life has been eventless and monotonous; like other boys of my class, I was five years at school at Eton, four years at college at Oxford; I never cared for any pursuit, sport, or study as a youngster, except poetry, riding, and swimming; and, though as a boy my verses were bad enough, I believe I may say I was far from bad at the two latter. Also, being bred by the sea, I was a good cragsman, and am vain to this day of having scaled a well-known cliff on the South Coast; ever before and ever since reputed to be inaccessible. Perhaps I may be forgiven for referring to such puerilities, having read (in cuttings from more than one American journal) bitterly contemptuous remarks upon my physical debility and puny proportions. I am much afraid this looks like an echo of poor great Byron's notorious and very natural soreness about his personal defect; but really, if I were actually of powerless or deformed body I am certain I should not care though all men (and women) on earth knew and remarked on it. I write all this rubbish because I really don't know what to tell you about myself, and having begun to egotise I go on in pure stupidity. I suppose you do not require a Rousseau-like record of my experiences in spiritual or material emotions; and knowing as you do the dates and sequence of my published books you know every event of my life. (*Note:* The order of composition is not always that of publication. *Atalanta* was begun the very day after I had given the last touch to *Chastelard.*)

*   *   *   *   *   *

Here I left off last night, being very tired and feeling myself getting stupid. I see I have already done much more than answer such of your questions as I could; and as you have induced me for the very first time in my life to write about myself, I am tempted, considering that I have probably been more be-written and belied than any man since Byron, to pour myself out to a sincere (distant) friend a little more, telling any small thing that may come into my head to mention.

I have heard that Goethe, Victor Hugo, and myself were all born in the same condition—all but dead, and certainly not expected to live an hour. Yet I grew up a healthy boy enough and fond of the open air, though slightly built, and have never had a serious touch of illness in my life. As for the sea, its salt *must* have been in my blood before I was born. I can remember no earlier enjoyment than being held up naked in my father's arms and brandished between his hands, then shot like a stone from a sling through the air, shouting and laughing with delight, head foremost into the coming wave—which could only have been the pleasure of a very little fellow. I remember being afraid of other things, but never of the sea. But this is enough of infancy; only it shows the *truth* of my endless passionate returns to the sea in all my verse.

—*Algernon Charles Swinburne*

THE POET

The poet in a golden clime was born,
  With golden stars above;
Dower'd with the hate of hate, the scorn of scorn,
  The love of love.

He saw thro' life and death, thro' good and ill,
  He saw thro' his own soul.
The marvel of the everlasting will,
  An open scroll,

Before him lay: with echoing feet he threaded
  The secretest walks of fame:
The viewless arrows of his thoughts were headed
  And wing'd with flame,

Like Indian reeds blown from his silver tongue,
  And of so fierce a flight,
From Calpe until Caucasus they sung,
  Filling with light

And vagrant melodies the winds which bore
  Them earthward till they lit;
Then, like the arrow-seeds of the field flower,
  The fruitful wit

Cleaving, took root, and springing forth anew
  Where'er they fell, behold,
Like to the mother plant in semblance, grew
  A flower all gold,

And bravely furnish'd all abroad to fling
  The winged shafts of truth,
To throng with stately blooms the breathing spring
  Of Hope and Youth.

So many minds did gird their orbs with beams,
  Tho' one did fling the fire.
Heaven flow'd upon the soul in many dreams
  Of high desire.

Thus truth was multiplied on truth, the world
  Like one great garden show'd,
And thro' the wreaths of floating dark upcurl'd,
  Rare sunrise flow'd.

And Freedom rear'd in that august sunrise
  Her beautiful bold brow,
When rites and forms before his burning eyes
  Melted like snow.

There was no blood upon her maiden robes
  Sunn'd by those orient skies;
But round about the circles of the globes
  Of her keen eyes

And in her raiment's hem was traced in flame
  WISDOM, a name to shake
All evil dreams of power—a sacred name.
  And when she spake,

Her words did gather thunder as they ran,
  And as the lightning to the thunder
Which follows it, riving the spirit of man,
  Making earth wonder,

So was their meaning to her words. No sword
  Of wrath her right arm whirl'd,
But one poor poet's scroll, and with *his* word
  She shook the world.

                                    —*Alfred Tennyson*

THE POET'S MIND

I

Vex not thou the poet's mind
    With thy shallow wit:
Vex not thou the poet's mind;
    For thou canst not fathom it.
Clear and bright it should be ever,
Flowing like a crystal river;
Bright as light, and clear as wind.

II

Dark-brow'd sophist, come not near;
    All the place is holy ground;
    Hollow smile and frozen sneer
    Come not here.
    Holy water will I pour
    Into every spicy flower
Of the laurel-shrubs that hedge it around.
The flowers would faint at your cruel cheer.
    In your eye there is death,
    There is frost in your breath
    Which would blight the plants.
        Where you stand you cannot hear
            From the groves within
            The wild-bird's din.
In the heart of the garden the merry bird chants.
It would fall to the ground if you came in.

In the middle leaps a fountain
   Like sheet lightning,
   Ever brightening
With a low melodious thunder;
All day and all night it is ever drawn
   From the brain of the purple mountain
   Which stands in the distance yonder:
It springs on a level of bowery lawn,
And the mountain draws it from Heaven above,
And it sings a song of undying love;
And yet, tho' its voice be so clear and full,
You never would hear it; your ears are so dull;
So keep where you are: you are foul with sin;
It would shrink to the earth if you came in.

                 —*Alfred Tennyscn*

THE POET'S SONG

The rain had fallen, the Poet arose,
   He pass'd by the town and out of the street,
A light wind blew from the gates of the sun,
   And waves of shadow went over the wheat,
And he sat him down in a lonely place,
   And chanted a melody loud and sweet,
That made the wild-swan pause in her cloud,
   And the lark drop down at his feet.

The swallow stopt as he hunted the fly,
   The snake slipt under a spray,
The wild hawk stood with the down on his beak,

And stared, with his foot on the prey,
And the nightingale thought, "I have sung many songs,
　But never a one so gay,
For he sings of what the world will be
When the years have died away."

　　　　　　　　　　　　—Alfred Tennyson

"A Serenade" from "Troubadour."

A few fairly cheerful days followed. Krimmie had saved enough money to see him through the summer— usually the most arid financial period—and, now that he was free to cultivate his own moods once more, he would have abundant tranquillity for the development of his latest idea: the application of a melodic and harmonic test to the small group of poems in free form he had gathered together. Strumming the mandolute, improvising backgrounds in accordance with the atmosphere of a poem, he would go over the syllables in his line divisions, add some here, clip others there, until the words and sounds seemed as true to each other as he could make them, and a balance of meaning and movement had been attained throughout. Before he was conscious of the trend of his activity, one of the backgrounds, starting with a casual improvisation, had attached itself to one of the poems; each time he read the lines, the music echoed the same clear accompaniment. He was thrilled with this compositional kinship. Laboring with feverish enthusiasm, he now tested the music by an application of the words to each note and chord, and then *vice versa,* backward and forward, until the first of the tone-poems had shaped itself beyond per-adventure. It was a serenade.

In his joyous trance, he shoved all the objects in the room against the walls and paced up and down the path, chanting the words and twanging the accompaniment. "I've got it!" he cried to himself. Possessed in every fibre, he stamped and swayed to the changing rhythm and awkwardly applied a pantomimic test. "I can see two dancers interpreting it!" Emotionally exhausted, he sat down on the couch, laid the instrument aside, buried his head in his hands and tried to see the dancers more distinctly.

—Alfred Kreymborg

THE DEAR MYSTERY

Joy, and the triumph and the doom of gladness
Make in my breast a music sweet as sadness;
Shall I not sing for sorrow, and again
Cry out, for the sheer joyousness of pain!
For all life's moods go murmuring like strings
In a low chord, and all things sound all things,
Through alternations of the grave and glad:
Yet, in the end, all things are grave and sad.
I feel all things, but cannot comprehend;
And run, laughing and weeping, to the end
Of the dear mystery, the fated race
And the deep darkness covers up my face.

—John Hall Wheelock

TRELAWNEY LIES BY SHELLEY

Trelawney lies by Shelley, and one bed
Of violets covers Keats and Severn, so
The friends who went life's way together know
No parting of the ways now they are dead.
Young Shelley, like a spirit, spoke and fled,
And Keats, before his youth began to blow;
Trelawney counted eighty winters' snow,
And eighty winters fell on Severn's head.
Yet here they lie, like poppies at one stroke
Cut by the selfsame blade in the summer sun,
The poets, and the friends who heard their song,
Believed and waited till the morning broke,
Then told their candle that the night was done;
When Friendship in the daytide rested, strong.

Charles L. O'Donnell, C.S.C.

From "Life, Letters and Literary Remains of John Keats," by Milnes.

The fifth canto of Dante pleases me more and more; it is that one in which he meets with Paulo and Francesca. I had passed many days in rather a low state of mind, and in the midst of them I dreamt of being in that region of Hell. The dream was one of the most delightful enjoyments I ever had in my life; I floated about the wheeling atmosphere, as it is described, with a beautiful figure, to whose lips mine were joined, it seemed for an age; and in the midst of all this cold and darkness I was warm; ever-flowery treetops sprung up, and we rested on them, sometimes with the lightness of a cloud, till the wind blew us away again. I tried a Sonnet on it: there are fourteen lines in it, but nothing of what I felt. Oh! that I could dream it every night.

—*John Keats*

From "Works of Robert Burns." To Mrs. Riddell.

I will wait on you, my ever-valued friend, but whether in the morning I am not sure. Sunday closes a period of our curst revenue business, and may probably keep me employed with my pen until noon. Fine employment for a poet's pen! There is a species of the human genus that I call the *gin-horse class:* what enviable dogs they are! Round, and round, and round they go—Mundell's ox that drives his cotton-mill is their exact prototype—without an idea or wish beyond their circle; fat, sleek, stupid, patient, quiet and contented; while here I sit altogether November-ish, a d—mnd melange of fretfulness and melancholy; not enough of the one to rouse me to passion, nor of the other to repose me in torpor; my soul flouncing and fluttering round her tenement, like a wild finch, caught amid the horrors of winter, and newly thrust into a cage. Well, I am persuaded that it was of me the Hebrew sage prophesied, when he foretold—"And behold, on whatsoever this man doth set his heart, it shall not prosper!" If my resentment is awakened, it is sure to be where it dare not squeak——

Pray that Wisdom and Bliss be more frequent visitors of

—Robert Burns

From "Introduction to the Works of Milton," by Corson.

. . . And long it was not after, when I was confirmed in this opinion, *that he who would not be frustrate of his hope to write well hereafter in laudable things, ought himself to be a true poem; that is, a composition and pattern of the best and honourablest things; not presuming to sing high praises of heroic men, or famous cities, unless he have in himself the experience and the practice of all that which is praiseworthy.*

—John Milton

IF THEY WILL NOT HEAR ME

If they will not hear me, shall I sing another song,
  Louder yet, or longer, or livelier to-day?
Shall I steal a passion that my music may be strong?
  Shall I steal a frolic that my music may be gay?

Thrushes sing their own song over again and over;
  Larks sing their own song wherever they may fly;
Robins sing their own song, hopping in the clover
  Of my cool, wet lawn. Are they braver than I?

—Marguerite Wilkinson

CONCERNING CHAUCER

Chaucer describes himself in the Prologue to Sir
Thopas in "The Canterbury Tales" as a chubby, retiring,
but observant personage with something roguish in his
face; though possibly the word *elfish* does not mean mis-
chievous, but dreamy, as if bewitched by elves.

> Whan seyd was al this miracle, every man
> As sobre was that wonder was to se,
> Til that oure Hooste japen tho bigan,
> And thanne at erst he looked upon me,
> And seyde thus: 'What man artow?' quod he;
> 'Thou lookest as thou woldest fynde an hare;
> For ever upon the ground I se thee stare.
> Approche neer, and looke up murily.
> Now war yow, sires, and lat this man have place;
> He in the waast is shape as wel as I;
> This were a popet in an arm tenbrace
> For any womman, smal and fair of face.
> He semeth elvyssh by his contenaunce,
> For unto no wight dooth he daliaunce.

He gives another picture of himself in "The House of
Fame" when he is conversing with the eagle that is carrying the poor poet in his claws through the air. The eagle
tells him that Jove appreciates his long service.

> That thou so longe trewely
> Hast served so ententifly
> His blinde nevew Cupido,
> And fair [dame] Venús also,
> Withoute guerdoun ever yit,
> And neverthelesse hast set thy wyt—
> Although that in thy heed ful lyte is—
> To make bookes, songes, or dytees,

In ryme, or elles in cadence,
As thou best canst in reverence
Of Love, and of his servants eke,
That have his servyse soght, and seke;
And peynest thee to preyse his arte,
Although thou haddest never part;
Wherfor, al-so God me blesse,
Joves halt hit greet humblesse,
And vertu eek, that thou wolt make
A-nyght ful ofte thyn heed to ake,
In thy studie so thou writest,
And evermo of love enditest,
In honour of him and preisynges,
And in his folkes furtherynges,
And in hir matere al devysest,
And noght him nor his folk despisest,
Although thou maist go in the daunce
Of hem that him list not avaunce.
'Wherfor, as I seyde, y-wys,
Jupiter considereth wel this;
And also, beau sir, other thynges;
That is, that thou hast no tydynges
Of Loves folk, if they be glade,
Ne of nothyng elles that God made;
And noght only fro fer contree,
That ther no tydyng cometh to thee,
But of thy verray neyghebores
That dwellen almost at thy dores,
Thou herest neither that ne this;
For when thy labour doon al is,
And hast y-maad thy rekenynges,
In stede of reste and newé thynges,
Thou gost hoom to thy hous anoon,
And, also domb as any stoon,
Thou sittest at another boke,
Til fully daswed is thy looke,
And lyvest thus as an heremyte,
Although thyn abstynence is lyte.

You see this shows a middle-aged poet going home from his figuring in the Custom House all the day long to study and write far into the night. There is even a hint in "The House of Fame" that Chaucer's wife was not altogether pleased with his way of living, for when the eagle called on Chaucer to awake, it was in the very voice and tone of one whom he might name, but refrains, with the exception that it was amiably said rather than the reverse. Chaucer was in fact a very close student and modestly insists that whatever good there may be in his writings comes out of the books of other men, as in this passage from the close of "Troilus and Criseyde."

> —Go, litel book! Go, litel myn tragédie!
> Ther God thy maker yit, or-that he dye,
> So sende might to make in som comédie!
> But, litel book, no making thou n'envýe,
> But subgit be to alle poesye!
> And kis the steppes wher-as thou seest pace
> Virgíle, Ovíde, Omér, Lucán, and Stace!
>
> And, for ther is so gret diversité
> In Englissh and in writing of our tonge,
> So prey to God that non miswrite thee,
> Ne thee mismetre for defaute of tonge!
> And, red wher-so thou be or elles songe,
> That thou be understonde God biseche!—
> But yet to purpos of my rather speche.

The honor he pays to the classic poets blends with his concern that the scribes—for this was before the day of printing—do not mangle his metre. Another expression of his modesty comes in the beginning of Book III in "The House of Fame" in his invocation to Apollo.

(The Invocation)

O god of science and of light,
Apollo, through thy grete myght,
This lytel laste book thou gye!
Nat that I wilne, for maistrýe
Here art poetical be shewed;
But, for the rym is light and lewed,
Yit make hit sumwhat agreable,
Thogh som vers faile in a sillable;
And that I do no diligence,
To shewe craft, but o sentence.
And if, divyne vertu, thou
Wilt helpe me to shewe now
That in myn hede y-marked is,—
Lo, that is for to menen this,
The Hous of Fame for to descryve,—
Thou shalt see me go as blyve
Unto the nexte laure I see,
And kisse it, for hit is thy tree.
Now entreth in my breste anoon!

Most appealing of all is that beautiful passage in the
opening of the "Legend of Good Women" in which
Chaucer declares his devotion to old books to be so great
that only the spring-time can win him from them.

A thousande tymes I have herd men telle,
That there is joy in hevene, and peyne in helle,
And I acorde wel that it is so;
But, natheles, yet wot I wel also,
That ther is noon dwellyng in this countree,
That eythir hath in hevene or in helle y-be,
Ne may of hit noon other weyes witen,
But as he hath herd seyde, or founde it writen;
For by assay ther may no man it preve.
But God forbede but men shulde leve

Wel more thing than men han seen with eye!
Men shal not wenen everything a lye
But-if hymselfe it seeth, or elles dooth;
For, God wot, thing is never the lasse sooth,
Thogh every wight ne may it not y-see.
Bernarde, the monke, ne saugh nat al, parde!
    Than mote we to bokes that we fynde,—
Thurgh which that olde thinges ben in mynde,—
And to the doctrine of these olde wyse,
Yeve credence, in every skylful wise,
That tellen of these olde appreved stories,
Of holynesse, of regnes, of victories,
Of love, of hate, of other sondry thynges,
Of whiche I may not maken rehersynges.
And if that olde bokes were awey,
Y'lorne were of remembraunce the key.
Wel ought us, thanne, honóuren and beleve
These bokes, ther we han noon other preve.
    And as for me, though that I konne but lyte,
On bokes for to rede I me delyte,
And to hem yive I feyth and ful credence,
And in myn herte have hem in reverence
So hertely, that ther is game noon
That fro my bokes maketh me to goon,
But it be seldom on the holyday,
Save, certeynly, whan that the month of May
Is comen, and that I here the foules synge,
And that the floures gynnen for to sprynge,—
Farewel my boke, and my devocion!

A little later on he says that he knows well earlier poets
have reaped the poetic field before him, taking away the
corn and leaving only chance ears for him to glean. Later
on in this Prologue, we have the very loveliest picture of
Chaucer down on his knees on a May-day morn watching
the opening of the little English daisy.

And doun on knees anon-right I me sette,
And, as I coude, this fresshe flour I grette;
Kneling alwey, til hit unclosed was,
Upon the smale softe swote gras.

There is an interesting passage in "The House of Fame"
in which he shows indifference to his own renown:

With that I gan aboute wende,
For oon that stood right at my bak,
Me thoughte goodly to me spak,
And seyde, 'Frend, what is thy name?
Artow come hider to han fame?'
'Nay, for-sothe, frend!' quod I;
'I cam noght hider, graunt mercy!
For no swich cause, by my heed!
Sufficeth me, as I were deed,
That no wyght have my name in honde.
I woot my-self best how I stonde.
For what I drye or what I thynke,—
I wol my selven al hit drynke,
Certeyn for the more part,
As ferforthe as I can myn art.'

There are three lines of Chaucer which, though dealing
with love, have in them the cry of the artist.

The lyf so short, the craft so long to lerne,
Th' assay so hard, so sharp the conquering,
The dredful Ioye, that alwey slit so yerne.

The poem on Truth known as the "Balade de bon conseyl"
gives a glimpse into the depths of his spiritual faith:

"Flee fro the prees, and dwelle with sothfastnesse,
Suffyce unto thy good, though hit be smal
For hord hath hate, and climbing tikelnesse,
Prees hath envye, and wele blent overal;
Savour no more than thee bihove shal;

Werk wel thy-self, that other folk canst rede;
And trouthe shal delivere, hit is no drede.

Tempest thee noght al croked to redresse,
In trust of hir that turneth as a bal: [Fortune]
Gret reste stant in litel besinesse;
And eek be war to sporne ageyn an al;
Stryve noght, as doth the crokke with the wal.
Daunte thy-self, that dauntest otheres dede;
And trouthe shal delivere, hit is no drede.

That thee is sent, receyve in buxumnesse,
The wrastling for this worlde axeth a fal.
Her nis non hoom, her nis but wildernesse:
Forth, pilgrim, forth! Forth, beste, out of thy stal!
Know thy contree, look up, thank God of al;
Hold the hye way, and lat thy gost thee lede:
And trouthe shal delivere, hit is no drede.''

—*Katharine Lee Bates*

HAPLESS

Hapless, hapless, I must be
All the hours of life I see,
Since my foolish nurse did once
Bed me on her leggen bones;
Since my mother did not weel
To snip my nails with blades of steel.
Had they laid me on a pillow
In a cot of water willow,
Had they bitten finger and thumb,
Not to such ill hap I had come.

—Walter de la Mare

THE POET'S TRAVAIL

In every generation a few persons ask by what throes genius is enabled to bear fruit. They would know what relationship exists between the human spirit and its achievements. William Butler Yeats has given his answer to this question most concisely in five lines of the poem called *"Ego Dominus Tuus"*:

> I call to the mysterious one who yet
> Shall walk the wet sand by the water's edge,
> And look most like me, being indeed my double,
> And prove of all imaginable things
> The most unlike, being my anti-self.

He has explained his theory at greater length in a small book published about seven years ago and called "Per Amica Silentia Lunæ."

The argument of the book, if such serene and simple speech can be called argument, is founded on the belief that the artist is the man who succeeds in giving expression to a self that is the antithesis of his everyday self. Mr. Yeats says:

When I think of any great poetical writer of the past, I comprehend, if I know the lineaments of his life, that the work is the man's flight from his entire horoscope, his blind struggle in the network of the stars.

And again,

Landor topped us all in calm nobility when the pen was in his hand, as in the daily violence of his passion when he laid it down.

And he believes that Keats was born with a thirst for luxury which he was never able "to slake with beautiful and strange objects" and therefore created an imaginary luxuriance.

The theory is one that might easily be misinterpreted and become a menace to talented youth. It would seem comic in a crude mind and ridiculous in the mouth of the unwary. Must a man be a felon to praise honesty in his verse, or a poltroon to exalt honor? Or conversely, will the strong and virtuous person necessarily write weak and base poetry? Must we alter the words of Christ and look for figs only among the coarse spines of the thistle? These are questions which, lacking discernment, or leisure for thought about complex psychological processes, we might be tempted to ask.

Yet the doctrine of the antithetical self may be better founded than such casual and inapt questioning would seem to suggest. It is not very remote, after all, from certain other doctrines current among plain people everywhere. What country parson has not told his flock to conquer faults by setting up the opposite virtues in their stead? What nation is without a saw or catchword showing that we desire and admire what we do not already possess? And modern psychology tells us that "every organism abhors incompleteness."

In his interesting "Psychology and Morals" Dr. J. A. Hadfield describes this urge of the partial personality towards completeness in a way which is pertinent in any discussion of Mr. Yeats' theory of genius:

The hunger of the soul for fulfillment is evidenced in *dreams*. We realize in dreams what we cannot realize in life: we complete ourselves in our dreams. Thus, the child in the slums dreams of gorgeous meals, because in reality it lacks food: on the other hand, the middle-class boy, with ample food, but dressed in collar and "bowler" hat, dreams of being a pirate or red Indian chief.

The dreams of adults follow the same law as the day-dreams of children, though they are more symbolic in character: they are compensating, complementary to conscious life. . . .

The completeness of the self can only be produced by the harmony of all the sentiments and complexes into one whole, the attainment of which we call *self-realization,* and the affective state of which we call happiness.

Self-realization—that is to say, the complete and full expression of all the instincts and impulses within us— cannot be achieved as long as there are elements in our soul that are repressed and denied expression. In a fully realized self there will be no conflict of purpose, no complexes, no repression, but the harmonious expression of all the vital forces towards a common purpose and end. That end, which is capable of so diverting the instincts from their original ends and redirecting them to the common purpose, we call the *ideal;* whilst the movement and activity of the self towards its realization we call *the will.* It is the craving for completeness and self-realization which urges us from the mere exhibition of our lusts and passions, and impels us to moral endeavor and the development of character. So, throughout the whole realm of organic life, in biology, psychology, morality, and religion, the craving for fulfillment . . . is the most potent force which drives us to live and strive with persistent energy, till the ultimate goal of self-realization is reached.

If indeed the urge to completeness is operative throughout the whole realm of organic life, in biology, psychology, morals, and religion, we may well believe that it is operative in æsthetics also, and in all the creative processes of art. If this be a fact, Mr. Yeats' theory is not only plausible, but probable.

Moreover, he does not state the theory too baldly. He modifies it greatly when he says:

The other self, the anti-self, or antithetical self, as we may choose to name it, comes but to those who are no longer deceived, whose passion is reality.

The winning of the power to express this anti-self, then, is not cheap, but costly. The thews of the spirit must be made strong by pulling against the current, not by drifting with it. As he says again:

We make out of the quarrel with others, rhetoric, but of the quarrel with ourselves, poetry.

Probably there is more rhetoric than poetry in the world because it is easier and pleasanter to quarrel with others than it is to quarrel with ourselves—and less humiliating!

The throes of dark inward battles may be the sharpest of all that belong to the poetic travail—we do not know, for these things have never been measured. One thing is sure—that by internal conflict our emotions are sublimated and refined, dissociated from their crude origins and associated with noble, delicate and subtle objectives. Our gracious mystic, Anna Hempstead Branch, says:

Many a temptation overcome creates a noble song and I suspect if we better understood the fine organisms of these living creatures—our poems—we would perceive that many a poem is in itself a fight. But not all.

Perhaps by their own interior tumults and agonies poets learn how to tell the world that all human love and grief are sacred, even in the harlot, even in the thief.

Psychologists talk, nowadays, of introverts and extraverts. A poet is both in an amazing fashion and to a surprising degree. His spiritual eye looks inward with sharpest scrutiny, suffering the vision of his own self to humble, touch, appall, divert, convict, torture and amuse him according to the changes of his moods and the diversity of the materials out of which they are made. But all the time, while he is peering in upon himself, he is gazing out towards the horizon, up towards the zenith; wandering up and down the highways of the universe. He feels his own times as other citizens do not feel them, for they are using them for practical purposes and he is seeking to fathom and to master them in creation. That may be why Mr. Yeats tells us that every great book exists in many minds before it is ever written through the effort of one. That may be why some poets believe that the individual subconscious life is one with a vast, racial, eternal subconscious life, so that all who live on the same plane share, even though they do not realize it, in a communion which may become the communion of saints. Again, that may be why a number of the best poets now living think that not a few poems are prophetic, foreshadowing and forelighting the ways that their makers will take and the goals that they will reach. Richard Le Gallienne sums it up nobly when he says, ''All the great men are of one mind.''

It is an easy matter for anybody who knows poets to understand why they cannot obey the injunction of tepid piety to ''look up and not down, look out and not in, and lend a hand.'' If he is to be more than a dilettante, he must look up, down, inside, outside, across, over, under and through, and, having looked again and again, his heart must follow his extended hand. This belongs to his travail.

People sometimes wonder how it is that a poet, who seems to be more sensitive than his neighbors personally, can bear to sing out before the whole world the deep and intimate secrets of his heart. It is, I think, only because the experience has been lived and relived over and over again in the poet's mind and related to numerous other experiences real and imaginary before he ever puts it into poetry. A poem is not a raw immediate emotion, not a crude reaction to any one set of circumstances taken alone. Whatever it is that stimulates the mind to the making of a poem on a certain theme is merely the occasion of its production, not the cause. Before any event in a poet's life has been made into valid poetry it must have been *felt through* and *thought out* in numerous ways, and colored by association with countless other things kept in his mind. Therefore, the poem, the finished work of a creative artist, is far removed from the event or emotion that may have given rise to it, and the poet can afford to regard it with detachment. This is how the unique becomes the universal.

Another part of a poet's difficulty has to do with the mundane matter of keeping himself physically alive in a world that God made for poets before man made it over for business. He wishes to make great poems. In order to do it he must eat, sleep, be clad, and have shelter for at least a part of his time. Yet, if he spends as much time as he should, and as he would, on meditation and the making of poetry, he will have no time to earn what is called "a living." And if he earns a living in the usual respectable way of the grocer and broker he will become less and less fit for the service of the Muse and will probably forego the chance of making a masterpiece. Keats wisely decided that half a day (and that is more than most poets are able to give) was not enough for poetry, that it rightly required the whole day of the poet.

The usual glib reply to this remark is to the effect that nobody can be "writing poems" all day and every day. And that is true. But when a poet is not actually engaged in setting down words on paper he should be thinking, reading, observing people and things, or meditating on all the rich thoughts and feelings that have entered into his life—in short, he should be living. One reason why poets often produce lovely lyrics in their youth and then become dull, decadent, or derivative in middle age is to be found simply in this fact that life insists that they shall earn a living, but will not allow them to live so fully and finely that growth is possible.

Another reply that is just as glib, and almost as usual, is to the effect that if ministers and school teachers do not complain of their small salaries, why should poets complain of their poverty? To which query we may make answer that there is a great difference between earning even a very small wage for doing the work which one believes he is called to do, and earning no wage at all unless one is willing to give up the dearest of all vocations. That very gradual ripening of the intellectual powers which Keats considered important for the poet is next to impossible for most of the young people who set out to be poets, because the leisure for any gradual ripening is far too expensive.

All the remedies for this condition of affairs are in Utopia. If we were to make laws obliging people to pay for their poetry at a fair rate, we should accomplish nothing, because we should have to leave it to their taste to decide what could be called poetry. And taste is even more scarce than discretion. If we should decide on a minimum wage for poets and attempt to organize them for their own protection, we should discover that they are all individualists, believers in the open shop, no matter how uneasy they are made by the law of supply and demand. The patronage of the ignorant is the abomination of desolation to them. Endowments can hardly be made with much wisdom until a poet's success is an established fact that wins him consideration, and then the endowment is not so greatly needed as in his youth. Prizes, as a rule, are pernicious. And, after all, the poet of heroic vision has a certain arrogance in his composition that does not admit of easy journeying on a royal road.

Very likely the only way is the highway, the way of the minstrels. Perhaps for ages yet to come poets should be content with wayfaring. And perhaps another order of St. Francis may even yet be formed of poets in love with Lady Poverty as much as with Lady Poetry, ready to spend days and nights with Brother Sun and Sister Moon, Brother Fire and Sister Water, depending in faith on the good will of God and man for all those small and pitiful necessities that poetry can seldom purchase. This was the way of Homer yesterday. It has been the way of Vachel Lindsay in our day. And to-morrow it may still be the way of innumerable singers yet unborn.

It is a greater thing to sleep on the rude earth than to toss in hotel bed paid for by people to whom poetry is nothing but one more way of being entertained. It is a better thing to eat berries under a bush than to exhibit your personality intimately in fifteen minutes to five hundred people for the sake of sharing their elaborate repast and perhaps making them wish to buy a few more books. It is holier and higher and more poetic to talk with birds and children and plain people by the roadside than it is to appear before dubious committees clad in purple and fine linen for the hope of winning a temporary vogue.

ODE

Bards of Passion and of Mirth,
Ye have left your souls on earth!
Have ye souls in heaven, too,
Double-lived in regions new?
Yes, and those of heaven commune
With the spheres of sun and moon;
With the noise of fountains wondrous,
And the parle of voices thunderous;
With the whisper of heaven's trees
And one another, in soft ease
Seated on Elysian lawns
Browsed by none but Dian's fawns;
Underneath large blue-bells tented,
Where the daisies are rose-scented,
And the rose herself has got
Perfume which on earth is not;

Where the nightingale doth sing
Not a senseless, tranced thing,
But divine melodious truth;
Philosophic numbers smooth;
Tales and golden histories
Of heaven and its mysteries.

Thus ye live on high, and then
On the earth ye live again;
And the souls ye left behind you
Teach us, here, the way to find you.
Where your other souls are joying,
Never slumber'd, never cloying.
Here, your earth-born souls still speak
To mortals, of their little week;
Of their sorrows and delights;
Of their passions and their spites;
Of their glory and their shame;
What doth strengthen and what maim.
Thus ye teach us, every day,
Wisdom, though fled far away.

Bards of Passion and of Mirth,
Ye have left your souls on earth!
Ye have souls in heaven, too,
Double-lived in regions news?

—*John Keats*

From **"Life, Letters and Literary** Remains of John Keats,"
by Milnes.

. . . I find I cannot exist without Poetry—without eternal Poetry; half the day will not do the whole of it. I

began with a little, but habit has made me a leviathan. I had become all in a tremble from not having written anything of late: the Sonnet over-leaf (*i.e.*, on the preceding page) did me good; I slept the better last night for it; this morning, however, I am nearly as bad again. Just now I opened Spenser, and the first lines I saw were these—

"The noble heart that harbors virtuous thought
And is with child of glorious great intent,
Can never rest until it forth have brought
Th' eternal brood of glory excellent."

—*John Keats*

From "Life, Letters and Literary Remains of John Keats," by Milnes. To Haydon.

. . . I suppose, by your telling me not to give way to forebodings, George has been telling you what I have lately said in my letters to him; truth is, I have been in such a state of mind as to read over my lines and to hate them. I am one that "gathereth samphire, dreadful trade": the cliff of Poetry towers above me; yet when my brother reads some of Pope's Homer, or Plutarch's Lives, they seem like music to mine. I read and write about eight hours a day. There is an old saying, "Well begun is half done"; 'tis a bad one; I would use instead, "Not begun at all till half done"; so, according to that, I have not begun my Poem, and consequently, *à priori*, can say nothing about it; thank God I do begin ardently, when I leave off, notwithstanding my occasional depressions, and I hope for the support of a high power while I climb this little eminence, and especially in my years of momentous labour. I remember your saying that you had notions of a good Genius presiding over you. I have lately had the same thought, for things which, done half at random, are afterwards confirmed by my judgment in a dozen features of propriety. Is it too of all sorts of irregularities. . . .

* * * * *

. . . But I cannot write while my spirit is fevered in a contrary direction, and I am now sure of having plenty of it this summer; at this moment I am in no enviable situation. I feel that I am not in a mood to write any to-day, and it appears that the loss of it is the beginning of all sorts of irregularities.

—*John Keats*

From "Life, Letters and Literary Remains of John Keats," by Milnes. To Hunt.

I went to the Isle of Wight, thought so much about poetry, so long together, that I could not get to sleep at night; and, moreover, I know not how it is, I could not get wholesome food. By this means, in a week or so, I became not over-capable in my upper stories, and set off pell-mell for Margate, at least a hundred and fifty miles, because, forsooth, I fancied I should like my old lodgings here, and could continue to do without trees. Another thing, I was too much in solitude, and consequently was obliged to be in continual burning of thought as an only resource. However, Tom is with me at present, and we are very comfortable. We intend, though, to get among some trees. How have you got on among them? How are the nymphs? I suppose they have led you a fine dance. Where are you now?

I have asked myself so often why I should be a Poet more than other men, seeing how great a thing it is, how great things are to be gained by it, what a thing to be in the mouth of Fame, that at last the idea has grown so monstrously beyond my seeming power of attainment, that the other day I nearly consented with myself to drop into a Phaeton. Yet 'tis a disgrace to fail even in a huge attempt, and at this moment I drive the thought from me. I begun my poem about a fortnight since, and have done some every day, except traveling ones. Perhaps I may have done a good deal for the time, but it appears such a pin's point to me, that I will not copy any out. When I consider that so many of these pin-points go to form a bodkin-point (God send I end not my life with a bare bodkin, in its modern sense) and that it requires a thousand bodkins to make a spear bright enough to throw any light to posterity, I see nothing but continual uphill journeying. Nor is there anything more unpleasant (it may come among the thousand and one) than to be so journeying and to miss the goal at last. But I intend to whistle all these cogitations into the sea, where I hope they will breed storms violent enough to block up all exit from Russia. . . .

—*John Keats*

From "Life, Letters and Literary Remains of John Keats," by Milnes. Letter to his publisher.

I am extremely indebted to you for your liberality in the shape of manufactured rag, value 20£, and shall immediately proceed to destroy some of the minor heads of that hydra the Dun; to conquer which the knight need have no sword, shield, cuirass, cuisses, herbadgeon, spear, casque, greaves, paldrons, spurs, chevron, or any other scaly commodity, but he need only take the Banknote of Faith and Cash of Salvation, and set out against the monster, invoking the aid of no Archimago or Urganda, but finger me the paper, light as the Sybil's leaves in Virgil, whereat the fiend skulks off with his tail between his legs. Touch him with this enchanted paper, and he whips you his head away as fast as a snail's horn; but then the horrid propensity he has to put it up again has discouraged many very valiant knights. He is such a never-ending, still-beginning sort of a body, like my landlady of the Bell. I think I could make a nice little allegorical poem, called "The Dun," where we would have the Castle of Carelessness, the Drawbridge of Credit, Sir Novelty Fashion's expedition against the City of Tailors, etc., etc. I went day by day at my poem for a month; at the end of which time, the other day, I found my brain so overwrought that I had neither rhyme nor reason in it, so was obliged to give up for a few days. I hope soon to be able to resume my work. I have endeavoured to do so once or twice; but to no purpose. Instead of poetry, I have a swimming in my head, and feel all the effects of a mental debauch, lowness of spirits, anxiety to go on, without the power to do so, which does not at all tend to my ultimate progression. However, to-morrow I will begin my next month. This evening I go to Canterbury, having got tired of Margate; I was not right in my head when I came. . . .

John Keats

From "Life, Letters and Literary Remains of John Keats," by Milnes.

. . . This morning I am in a sort of temper, indolent and supremely careless; I long after a stanza or two of Thomson's "Castle of Indolence," my passions are all asleep, from my having slumbered till nearly eleven, and weakened the animal fibre all over me, to a delightful sensation, about three degrees on this side of faintness. If I had teeth of pearl, and the breath of lilies, I should call it languor; but, as I am, I must call it laziness. In this state of effeminacy, the fibres of the brain are relaxed, in common with the rest of the body, and to such a happy degree, that pleasure has no show of enticement, and pain no unbearable frown; neither Poetry, nor Ambition, nor Love, have any alertness of countenance; as they pass by me, they seem rather like three figures on a Greek vase, two men and a woman, whom no one but myself could distinguish in their disguisement. This is the only happiness, and is a rare instance of advantage in the body overpowering the mind.

—John Keats

From "The Poet's Progress."

But O thou cruel stepmother and hard,
To thy poor, fenceless, naked child, the Bard!
A thing unteachable in worldly skill,
And half an idiot too, more helpless still:
No heels to bear him from the op'ning dun,
No claws to dig, his hated sight to shun:
No horns, but those by luckless Hymen worn,
And those, alas! not Amalthea's horn:
No nerves olfact'ry, true to Mammon's foot,
Or grunting, grub sagacious, evil's root:
The slly sheep that wanders wild astray,
Is not more friendless, is not more a prey;
Vampyre-booksellers drain him to the heart,
And viper-critics cureless venom dart.

—*Robert Burns*

From "Dryden's Letters." To his sons at Rome.

. . . In the meantime, I am writing a song for St.
Cecilia's Feast, who, you know, is the patroness of music.
This is troublesome, and no way beneficial; but I could
not deny the stewards of the feast, who came in a body to
me to desire that kindness, one of them being Mr. Bridg-
man, whose parents are your mother's friends. I hope to
send you thirty guineas between Michaelmas and Christ-
mas, of which I will give you an account when I come to
town.

—*John Dryden*

From "Introduction to the Works of Milton," by Corson. To Emeric Bigot.

Many have made a figure by their published writings whose living voice and daily conversation have presented next to nothing that was not low and common: if, then, I can attain the distinction of seeming myself equal in mind and manners to any writings of mine that have been tolerably to the purpose, there will be the double effect that I shall so have added weight personally to my wrtings, and shall receive back by way of reflection from them credit, how small soever it may be, yet greater in proportion. For, in that case, whatever is right and laudable in them, that same I shall seem not more to have derived from authors of high excellence than to have fetched forth pure and sincere from the inmost feelings of my own mind and soul. . . . Why, in truth, should I not bear gently the deprivation of sight, when I may hope that it is not so much lost as revoked and retracted inwards, for the sharpening rather than the blunting of my mental edge.

—*John Milton*

From "To my Friend Master John Fletcher, upon his Faithful Shepherdess."

I know too well, that, no more than the man
That travels through the burning Desarts, can
When he is beaten with the raging Sun,
Half smother'd in the dust, have power to run
From a cool River, which himself doth find,
E're he be slack'd; no more can he whose mind
Joyes in the Muses, hold from that delight,
When nature, and his full thoughts bid him write:

Yet wish I those whom I for friends have known,
To sing their thoughts to no ears but their own.
Why should the man, whose wit ne'r had a stain,
Upon the publick Stage present his [vein],
And make a thousand men in judgment sit,
To call in question his undoubted wit,
Scarce two of which can understand the laws
Which they should judge by, nor the parties cause?

[•]   [•]   [•]   •   •   •

—*Francis Beaumont*

From "Pope's Works."

. . . I believe no mortal ever lived in such indolence
and inactivity of body, though my mind be perpetually rambling—it no more knows whither than poor
Adrian's did when he lay a-dying. Like a witch, whose
carcass lies motionless on the floor, while she keeps her
airy sabbaths, and enjoys a thousand imaginary enter-
tainments abroad, in this world and in others, I seem to
sleep in the midst of the hurry, even as you would swear
a top stands still, when it is in the whirl of its giddy
motion. It is no figure, but a serious truth I tell thee,
when I say that my days and nights are so much alike,
so equally insensible of any moving power but fancy, that
I have sometimes spoke of things in our family as truths
and real accidents, which I only dreamt of; and again,
when some things that actually happened came into my
head, have thought, till I enquired, that I had only dreamed
of them.

—*Alexander Pope*

Pope to Wycherley.

. . . For as, when madmen are found incurable, wise
men give them their way, and please them as well as they
can, so, when those incorrigible things, poets, are once irre-
coverably bemused, the best both to quiet them, and secure
yourself from the effects of their frenzy, is to feed their
vanity: which, indeed, for the most part, is all that is fed
in a poet.

—Alexander Pope

From "Table Talk."

A. Such lofty strains embellish what you teach—
Mean you to prophesy, or but to preach?
B. I know the mind that feels indeed the fire
The Muse imparts and can command the lyre,
Acts with a force, and kindles with a zeal.
Whate'er the theme, that others never feel.
If human woes her soft attention claim,
A tender sympathy pervades the frame,
She pours a sensibility divine
Along the nerve of every feeling line.
But if a deed not tamely to be borne
Fire indignation and a sense of scorn,
The strings are swept with such a power, so loud,
The storm of music shakes th' astonsh'd crowd
So, when remote futurity is brought
Before the keen inquiry of her thought,
A terrible sagacity informs
The poet's heart; he looks to distant storms;

He hears the thunder ere the tempest lowers!
And, arm'd with strength surpassing human powers,
Seizes events as yet unknown to man,
And darts his soul into the dawning plan.
Hence, in a Roman mouth, the graceful name
Of prophet and of poet was the same;
Hence British poets, too, the priesthood shared,
And every hallowed Druid was a bard.

—*William Cowper*

Poetic excitement, when accompanied by protracted labour in composition, has throughout my life brought on more or less bodily derangement. Nevertheless, I am, at the close of my seventy-third year, in what may be called excellent health; so that intellectual labour is not necessarily unfavourable to longevity. But perhaps I ought here to add that mine has been generally carried on out of doors. . . .

A cheerful life is what the Muses love,
A soaring spirit is their prime delight.

—*William Wordsworth*

From "The Prelude."

And now it would content me to yield up
Those lofty hopes awhile, for present gifts
Of humbler industry. But, oh, dear Friend!
The Poet, gentle creature as he is,
Hath, like the Lover, his unruly times;
His fits when he is neither sick nor well,

Though no distress be near him but his own
Unmanageable thoughts: his mind, best pleased
While she as duteous as the mother dove
Sits brooding, lives not always to that end,
But like the innocent bird, hath goadings on
That drive her as in trouble through the groves;
With me is now such passion, to be blamed
No otherwise than as it lasts too long.

—William Wordsworth

From "Letters and Journals of Byron," by Moore. To his publisher.

I have not done a stitch of poetry since I left Switzerland, and have not at present the *estro* upon me. The truth is, that you are *afraid* of having a *Fourth* Canto *before* September, and of another copyright, but I have at present no thoughts of resuming that poem, nor of beginning any other. If I write, I think of trying prose, but I dread introducing living people, or applications which might be made to living people. Perhaps one day or other I may attempt some work of fancy in prose descriptive of Italian manners and of human passions; but, at present, I am preoccupied. As for poesy, mine is the *dream* of the sleeping passions; when they are awake, I cannot speak their language, only in their somnambulism, and just now they are not dormant. . . .

—Lord Byron

From "Works of Thomas Gray." To Richard West.

. . . Low spirits are my true and faithful companions; they get up with me, go to bed with me, make journeys and return as I do; nay, and pay visits, and will even affect to be jocose, and force a feeble laugh with me; but most commonly we sit alone, . . . the prettiest insipid company in the world. However, when you come, I believe they must undergo the fate of all humble companions, and be discarded. Would I could turn them to the same use that you have done, and make an Apollo of them. If they could write such verses with me, not hartshorn, nor spirit of amber, nor all that furnishes the closet of an apothecary's widow, should persuade me to part with them. . . .

—Thomas Gray

From "Letters of George Meredith." To the Rev. Augustus Jessop.

. . . It is true that I have fallen from what I once hoped to do. The fault is hardly mine. Do you know Vexation, the slayer? There is very little poetry to be done when one is severely and incessantly harassed. My nerves have given way under it, and it is only by great care and attention to the directions of my doctor that I can work at all. I have now more leisure and somewhat better health, and the result is, that I have gone back partially to my old mistress.

—George Meredith

From "On English Poetry."

It is intolerable to feel so bound compared with the freedom of a musician or a sculptor; in spite of the exactions of that side of the art, the poet cannot escape into mere rhythmic sound; there is always the dead load of sense to drag about with him. I have often felt I would like to be a painter at work on a still life, puzzling out ingenious relationships between a group of objects varying in form, texture and colour. Then when people came up and asked me: "Tell me, sir, is that a Spode jar?" or "Isn't that a very unusual variety of lily?" I would be able to wave them away placdly; the questions would be irrelevant. But I can't do that in poetry, everything *is* relevant; it is an omnibus of an art—a public omnibus.

—*Robert Graves*

From "The Strayed Reveller."
These things, Ulysses,
The wise bards also
Behold, and sing.
But oh, what labour!
O prince, what pain!
They, too, can see
Tiresias; but the gods,
Who give them vision,
Added this law:
That they should bear, too,
His groping blindness,
His dark foreboding,
His scorned white hairs;

Bear Hera's anger
Through a life lengthened
To seven ages.

They see the centaurs
On Pelion; then they feel,
They, too, the maddening wine
Swell their large veins to bursting; in wild pain
They feel the biting spears
Of the grim Lapithae, and Theseus drive,
Drive crashing through their bones; they feel,
High on a jutting rock in the red stream,
Alcmena's dreadful son
Ply his bow. Such a price
The gods exact for song:
To become what we sing.

They see the Indian
On his mountain lake; but squalls
Make their skiff reel, and worms
In the unkind spring have gnawn
Their melon-harvest to the heart. They see
The Scythian; but long frosts
Parch them in winter-time on the bare steppe,
Till they, too, fade like grass; they crawl
Like shadows forth in spring.

They see the merchants
On the Oxus-stream; but care
Must visit first them, too, and make them pale:
Whether, through whirling sand,

A cloud of desert robber-horse have burst
Upon their caravan; or greedy kings,
In the walled cities the way passes through,
Crushed them with tolls; or fever-airs,
On some great river's marge,
Mown them down, far from home.

They see the heroes
Near harbour; but they share
Their lives, and former violent toil in Thebes,—
Seven-gated Thebes, or Troy;
Or where the echoing oars
Of Argo first
Startled the unknown sea.

The old Silenus
Came, lolling in the sunshine,
From the dewy forest coverts
This way at noon.
Sitting by me, while his fauns
Down at the water-side
Sprinkled and smoothed
His drooping garland,
He told me these things.

But I, Ulysses,
Sitting on the warm steps,
Looking over the valley,
All day long, have seen,
Without pain, without labour,
Sometimes a wild-haired maenad,

Sometimes a faun with torches,
And sometimes, for a moment,
Passing through the dark stems
Flowing-robed, the beloved,
The desired, the divine,
Beloved Iacchus.

Ah, cool night-wind, tremulous stars!
Ah, glimmering water,
Fitful earth-murmur,
Dreaming woods!
Ah, golden-haired, strangely smiling goddess
And thou, proved, much-enduring,
Wave-tossed wanderer!
Who can stand still?
Ye fade, ye swim, ye waver before me—
The cup again!

Faster, faster,
O Circe, goddess,
Let the wild, thronging train,
The bright procession
Of eddying forms,
Sweep through my soul!

—*Matthew Arnold*

From "Letters." To Mrs. Forster.

Kingsley's remarks were very *handsome,* especially coming from a brother in the craft. I should like to send you a letter which I had from Froude about *Merope,* just at the same time that your record of Kingsley's criticisms reached me. If I can find it when I return to England I will send it to you. It was to beg me to discontinue the *Merope* line, but entered into very interesting developments, as the French say, in doing so. Indeed, if the opinion of the general public about my poems were the same as that of the leading literary men, I should make more money by them than I do. But, more than this, I should gain the stimulus necessary to enable me to produce my best—all that I have in me, whatever that may be—to produce which is no light matter with an existence so hampered as mine is. People do not understand what a temptation there is, if you cannot bear anything not *very good,* to transfer your operations to a region where form is everything. Perfection of a certain kind may there be attained, or at least approached, without knocking yourself to pieces, but to attain or approach perfection in the region of thought and feeling, and to unite this with perfection of form, demands not merely an effort and a labour, but an actual tearing of oneself to pieces, which one does not readily consent to (although one is sometimes forced to it) unless one can devote one's whole life to poetry. Wordsworth could give his whole life to it, Shelley and Byron both could, and were besides driven by their demon to do so. Tennyson, a far inferior natural power to either of the three, can; but of the moderns Goethe is the only one, I think, of those who have had an *existence assujettie,* who has thrown himself with a great result into poetry. And even he felt what I say, for he could, no doubt, have done more, *poetically*, had he been freer; but it is not so light a matter, when you have other grave claims on your powers, to submit voluntarily to the exhaustion of the best poetical production in a time like this. Goethe speaks somewhere of the endless matters on which he had employed himself, and says that with the labour he had given to them he might have produced half a dozen more good tragedies; but to produce these, he says, I must have been *sehr zerrissen*. It is only in the best poetical epochs (such as the Elizabethans) that you can descend into yourself and produce the best of your thought and feeling naturally, and without an overwhelming and in some degree morbid effort; for then all the people around you are more or less doing the same thing. It is natural, it is the bent of the time to do it; its being the bent of the time, indeed, is what makes the time a *poetical* one.

—*Matthew Arnold*

SONGS I SANG LONG AGO

Songs I sang long ago
I would forget; I do not know
Why I sang shrilly, frailly,
Crudely, harshly, poorly, palely.
But the little song I sang last night
Is the song of my delight,
Dearest of all the songs of men,
And will be—till I sing again!

—*Marguerite Wilkinson*

When poems ripen into form,
Let them be harvested by a storm;
Let a great gale blow them down.
You will not find them late or soon
In orchards where such fruit should be,
But globes of amber out of the sea
Flung by the spinning black typhoon:
Apples of uncertainty:
An island pomegranate laced with brown:
A nectarine like a cloven moon.

—Grace Hazard Conkling

Art is a disciplining of some excitement of the mind.
It is a strong excitement in perfect control. It should be
an excitement about some permanent element in life. It
demands an eagerness of mind, and a balance or steadiness
of nature.

Beyond this it is difficult to go; except to say that it is
an exacting thing, like athletics, and demands good bodily
trim. The body is the machine by which the mind has to
work. The artist works better when he is in good condition. Some strange and very beautiful art has been
made by men suffering from disease; but the best art is
the work of superb health of mind and body; it is the
happy and healthy exercise of mental power.

—John Masefield

A CONVERSATION

The scene is Elysium. Fields of asphodel surround a spacious amphitheatre. Two persons are discovered standing on the steps, engaged in talk. One of them, an elderly gentleman of agreeable aspect and with a reedy voice, is clothed in a chiton. The other, a tall, handsome swarthy shade, wearing a suit of cinque-cento richness and elaborate gems, is a man of forty-three. The old Greek is called Plato, the middle-aged Florentine, Lorenzo, surnamed the Magnificent.

LORENZO: The most anarchic days in Florence hold no candle to the state of affairs down here. Per bacco! what we need is a tyrant, who could at least order a festival decently. They are forever wanting to celebrate the arrival of heroes newly dead, and all the talent in Hades is wasted for want of a leading spirit.

PLATO: Do these festivals really seem to you of so much importance? I had thought that having once met face to face, I could persuade you that what matters is not the life of art, but the art of life.

LORENZO: That's all very well for one who has never been coffined. But after we have once tasted the subterrene air we must admit that it is only art that endures past the grave itself. They tell me that more people have come to look at my tomb than ever studied you in the palace of the Medicis!

(Enter a third party—a rugged-faced ghost in a sack suit, with an old tam pulled over one ear and a musical score sticking out of one pocket.)

LORENZO *(hailing him)*: Hallo there, friend—Ricardo, is it?

WAGNER *(for it is indeed he, turning about and inspecting Lorenzo gravely)*: Richard Wagner, if you please.

Not that names matter very much down here: we are all dead together. And yet (*he pauses a moment, lost in an old revery*)—I have sometimes thought I could wake the departed to life if I could only find the right myth for a new music-drama. A myth as old as those of your Hellenes (*he glances toward Plato*) and still vivid with a sense of all we have learned since Jupiter and Jehovah surrendered to the Immanent Will whereof Schopenhauer wrote.

LORENZO: What barbarians you Germans are! No offense, of course. But I can't help thinking how few of you understand what our good Pico so eloquently taught—that in Christian Platonism theology and philosophy embrace like lovers. (*To Plato*) : Isn't that true, my friend?

PLATO (*gently putting this question aside for that which really interests him*) : I died before the Christ myth was born, but I understand that it produced longer wars than did the rape of Helen. What troubles me in this musician's talk is that he seems to think that the poet's business is with things untrue, and with evil things, like the quarrels of the gods.

WAGNER: No—oh, no. You mistake me. We must re-create the myth, which is fundamentally truer than any history, so that it will rouse a sense of wonder, an assenting emotion, as valid as anything felt by you Greeks before an Aeschylean tragedy, but richer by all the emotional values growing out of the new industrial and social order. But all this is only a dream. There is no public among us capable of responding to such an emotional stimulus. We are too separate for any such new and holy catharsis.

LORENZO: It is not the public that is wanting here. As

I was about to remark to Plato—Elysium is as unendurable as Milan or Naples because there is no one to manage things in an orderly fashion. If only we had such a patron as my grandfather, Cosimo, was in his day, and, in all modesty, as I tried to be in my own.

WAGNER: A patron, do you say? What good is a patron without a public? Even Ludwig of Bavaria, blessed be his memory, couldn't build the theatre for my music-dramas without the help of all the other "Wagnerians," from Cairo to St. Petersburg. Besides, the proper patron, as I discovered so late in life, is a king. A king is sur-rounded by a court. A court is a nest of intrigue, con-spiracy, cabal. . . . Ach! if one could but achieve a repub-lic of artists, governed by a tyrant——

LORENZO (interrupting triumphantly): Florence! Flor-ence under the Medicis! Didn't I say so!

PLATO: A republic governed by a tyrant? A republic of artists! What curious notions! Why, these artists would be so busy with their lutes and their pretty lies that they would never give a thought to virtue. Nor would they ever propagate. Their State would perish for want of citizens within two generations.

WAGNER (impatiently reverting to the question that chiefly agitates him): But how shall the artist be enabled to do his work? He can't depend on the mob. They don't want to hear him. He has too much on his shoulders: he must build not merely his own creations—and what a ter-rific task that is, you are better off not knowing—he must build up his very audience! A man must be more than a genius to go on under such conditions as that.

LORENZO: You are right. And yet, what a thing it is to

be a patron! Our family knew something about that side of it. One has to support any number of fools and idlers in the hope of finding one true artist. And then when you have him, all the other princes vie in trying to snatch him from you for their own glory. Besides, you have to give a Michelangelo, for instance, enough to keep his father and his brothers and their children into the bargain, and you are always being worried by his private affairs and his petty jealousies.

PLATO: If you must have artists, and I do not altogether share your feeling in the matter—is it not possible that they may be chosen in youth from among competitors by a jury of their peers, to be supported by the State, until they are recognized by their public?

WAGNER: A jury of his peers? Do you think Mendelssohn and Meyerbeer would have listened to the notion of supporting me long enough for me to have written a single bar of music? Why, I would rather trust a crowd of cooks and clerks than such men as that!

PLATO: Forgive me, but I don't understand you. You say a poet must be allowed freedom from the stress of earning his livelihood until he has accomplished so greatly that the crowd follows and exalts him; and then you say that his fellow bards are too dull or too small-minded to grant him those years of free apprenticeship. Who, then, is to choose among the young men pressing forward for their laurels, if neither the crowd nor his own colleagues know an artist when they see one? Would you, perhaps, leave it to the Guardians of the State?

WAGNER (*sighing*): If they were men of genius, yes.

PLATO: They should be of gold thrice-refined, in my Republic. But they would be concerned for the welfare of the State, not for that of a handful of deceived and deceiving myth-makers.

LORENZO: It is a real problem, this. We haven't even solved it in Elysium. We have the talent of the centuries at our command, and what have we done with it? And why has it been thus? Madonna mia! one might as well be alive!

WAGNER: Oh, don't say that! To be alive is to be forever worrying about bread and immortality. Here at least we have recovered the innocence of the unborn as to those questions. And yet, do you know, I would even suffer life again to be able to write another music-drama—greater than any I ever attempted on earth.

LORENZO: Who wouldn't, truly, be alive again—yes, dining with a Sforza or supping with an Aragonese, for the pleasure of tasting ambition on his tongue once more?

WAGNER: There's the rub, my Florentine! Ambition. The Philistines like to say, or did in my time, that if you deprive an artist of ambition by giving him the security of patronage, he will come to nothing.

LORENZO: And weren't they right in that? How many comfortable geniuses have you known?

WAGNER (after some reflection): There was Goethe.

LORENZO: Yes, and there was also a certain Da Vinci.

PLATO: Ambition is a carrot to be swung before a donkey. Your true poet, the one who will imitate noble actions for the enlightenment of all the folk, is one not to be moved by that sort of vegetable.

WAGNER: But even such a poet, concerned with ethics

rather than music, if you like, needs leisure, needs peace, needs his fallow season, if anything is to come of it.

LORENZO: And a tyrant is the one to grant him what he needs. If you can show me any period when the arts flourished more luxuriously than during the reign of my own house—well, then, I shall turn—what is that new word you taught me—turn socialist!

WAGNER: Perhaps all of us are right. Perhaps a jury composed in equal parts of artists and simple citizens and princes, or Guardians, would be the fairest in deciding which men deserve patronage of the State while their genius is in incubation.

LORENZO: Good! I accept the post of prince on your jury, and I shall call you in as the artist.

PLATO: But you have not decided who is to select the jury.

LORENZO: They will select themselves.

WAGNER: I can almost believe that.

LORENZO: But our plain citizen—who will he be? Say, Richard, shall we take in Plato to make our trio complete?

PLATO: You are very kind, but in all Elysium there is none less fitted for the post. Besides, no artist would listen to me for a moment.

LORENZO: An artist like Richard would (*appealing to Wagner*): wouldn't you?

WAGNER: Frankly, I would listen more readily to Schopenhauer. But I thought our third party was to be a Philistine?

PLATO: Oh, then don't choose a philosopher—the Philistines would never forgive you the slight put upon them by doing that.

LORENZO: Besides, Plato himself is a poet, though he does not acknowledge it. I foresee a difficult time for our jury.

WAGNER: No, no. We shall form it yet. (*With an inspiration*): Let us get hold of Meyerbeer!

—*Babette Deutsch*

THE DEPARTURE OF THE GOOD DÆMON

What can I do in Poetry,
Now the good Spirit's gone from me?
Why nothing now, but lonely sit,
And over-read what I have writ.

—*Robert Herrick*

THE PRIMARY INSPIRATION

"There is a widespread notion in the public mind that poetic inspiration has something mysterious and translunar about it, something which altogether escapes human analysis, which it would be almost sacrilege for analysis to touch. The Romans spoke of the poet's divine afflatus, the Elizabethans of his fine frenzy. And even in our own day critics, and poets themselves, are not lacking who take the affair quite as seriously."

With this paragraph for a beginning Conrad Aiken writes an interesting chapter on poetic inspiration for his book called "Scepticisms." He goes on to say that undoubtedly Freud has contributed something to our knowledge of the mechanism of inspiration. He also discusses and quotes "Le Mécanisme Cérébrale de la Pensée," by M. Nicolas Kostyleff, who, it seems, has made a study of the creative methods of a number of contemporary French poets. His theory is one of verbo-motor reactions. He believes that words, like other impressions, are stored in the mind with their chains of associations and that they are released, or, to quote Mr. Aiken, "begin automatically unravelling" when the poet is shocked into creation by some emotional stimulus. Probably it would be easy for M. Kostyleff, and for Mr. Aiken, to explain in this way much of the poetry of Shelley in which image seems to lead on to image and symbol to symbol merely by a process of association without much regard for relevancy in the structure of the poem.

This whole chapter in "Scepticisms" is a suggestive and stimulating explanation of the inexplicable. It is very sophisticated and sceptical. But near the end of it is a paragraph quite unlike the others, a paragraph remarkable for pathetic seriousness and wistful naïveté, in which Mr. Aiken admits that even Freud and M. Kostyleff seem to be strangely inadequate in their analysis of this thing that should not be called "mysterious and translunar." He says:

"It is to some deep hunger, whether erotic or not, or to some analogous compulsion, that we must look for the source of the power that sets in motion the delicate mechanism, on another plane, which M. Kostyleff has begun to illuminate for us. It is clear that this is not merely a sexual hunger, nor an æsthetic hunger, nor an ethical hunger, though all may have their place in it. . . . Is it merely in general the hunger of the frustrate (which we all are) for richer experience?"

When Mr. Aiken refers to "richer experience"—presumably to experience that asks more than sexual, æsthetic, or merely ethical satisfaction, we feel moved to answer as Confucius answered one of his disciples centuries ago. "Thou hast hit my meaning, Chang. Now I can talk of poetry to thee." For the phrase "richer experience" suggests all that great poets have found and expressed and the great fact of their inspiration, which does forever defy analysis, no matter how clearly we may be able later to analyze the method and the mechanism. When I study

the lives and writings of the masters I do indeed find them
taking the "affair" of inspiration "quite seriously."

I find Spenser speaking of poetry as "no arte, but a
divine gift and heavenly instinct." I find Shelley, who
was said to be an atheist in his time, invoking "intellectual
beauty" as a deified abstraction. The pensive and iambic
Wordsworth appeals to the "wisdom and spirit of the universe." Emerson describes "the universal nature," the
"world-soul" and "the over-soul." Yeats refers to the
racial memory which could hardly exist without a world-
soul or over-soul. A. E. names "The King in His Beauty"
as the source of his singing. Blake asks, "What is the
Holy Ghost but an intellectual fountain?" Milton, Browning, and many, many others speak directly of God as a
Being responsible for inspiration. Coleridge goes further,
for he defines a primary and secondary imagination in the
poet and says that the primary imagination is "a repetition in the finite mind of the eternal act of creation in the
infinite I AM," and that the secondary imagination is an
echo of the primary. Many of the greatest poets seem
always to believe that when they create poetry they are
in touch with something or somebody other than themselves—the "more" of William James—that pours energy
into them or through them and gives them full utterance.

Just how this increment of power is given we do not
fully know. Perhaps complexes are released. Perhaps
verbo-motor reactions do take place. But whence comes
the fiery beauty and order that differentiates the released
complexes and reactions of the poet from those of others
and gives them eternal life in the world? How is it that
the poet himself believes that they have come from some

source outside of himself? We have more to do with than complexes or reactions. We have what Mr. Aiken calls the hunger of the frustrate for richer experience, and we have the satisfaction of that hunger, the recognition of the insurgent God in a man's soul! And we do know, also, that contemplation, an austere and intense concentration of mind, tends to yield up the maker to His Maker in this miracle of recognition.

Perhaps this takes place through what is now called "the subconscious," or perhaps, as has been suggested by writers who dislike the unpleasant associations that have been made with that word, there is a super-conscious through which God enters into the mind of man. It does not matter what we call it unless we are scientists bristling with definitions, for, after all, as yet it is all mere nomenclature, so little do we know about it. But the point to be remembered is this: it has seemed to many of the wisest and greatest persons who have ever lived that on one side at least of our minds—which side we cannot tell—we are exposed to the touch of a spiritual life eternal, invincible, and ravishingly sweet, a life that can, by discipline of the will and by the high longing called aspiration, be brought into our consciousness and held there for a little while, or be wrought into works of beauty that the world is loth to give up.

The agnostic may deny all this, to be sure. For him an uprush is an uprush and it is nothing more. He may honestly assert that poets merely think these things that have not, for that reason, any objective truth. Or he may do what Mr. Aiken has done—give a few possible explanations of mechanism and method and then go on wondering about a fact in which he refuses to recognize the "mysterious and translunar." God is very old and Freud is relatively new. Therefore, it is more fashionable just now to describe inspiration according to Freud than it is to find it according to God. One would think that God might constitute an hypothesis for consideration. He is needed even in that small way.

It is well to remember that God has not yet contradicted Freud, though science changes so rapidly nowadays that this may happen at any moment. On the other hand, if we assume that Freud and others have explained away God, how are we to account for the richer experience given to the great geniuses who believed in Him and given, apparently, only in answer to belief? Perhaps it is very fortunate for us that God does not object to science as much as a few scientists object to Him.

Perhaps Blake meant something like this when he said that "all things are of the poetic genius." Or, as Percy MacKaye says,

In the vast of night and its vacancy
I prayed aloud to Poetry,
And his luminous eyes grew large and dim
And my heart-pulse quickened to question him;

But if we can be so defiantly old-fashioned as to admit, with the belief of the greatest poets to support us, that God may be concerned in inspiration, we do not need to deny anything that scientists may be able to discover about the mechanism and the method. If the psychologists who study prayer in the believer would study also inspiration in the poet, much might be learned that would be of value to religion and to art, much that would make even stronger forces than they are at present in the life of mankind.

The great poet who believes that he finds his inspiration in God has at least one understanding neighbor in the great saint who finds his very life in prayer. Though they climb to their hilltop of light from opposite sides, the poet being concerned with holy beauty and the saint with the beauty of holiness, nevertheless they meet on the summit. They find the "rose of all roses, rose of all the world," and tell the color of it to mankind. This is their richer experience and though we never fully comprehend it, though it has meaning for us only in so far as we ourselves are also climbing, yet we listen and are glad. We are so glad that even in denying parts of their faith we inconsistently wish them to retain and reaffirm it. Forever the small company of the great and those who hunger and thirst after greatness are working their miracles for us. They visit in Heaven. They go to the great falls for their power, to the central fire for their heat. For them invocation is no literary convention, but a grand actuality.

The great poet is like the great saint, also, in being a creature of ecstasy. They two know as much as any souls that live of what happens when colors are swiftly reborn in color and tones in music, when time widens out suddenly into eternity, or when eternity is felt in a brief atom of time, when all visible lights become invisible and only that is seen which has glory for the inward angel. As much as any souls that live do they know of the burning bush of Moses and of the region where Alph, the sacred river, ran.

It may be said of ecstasy that, although it sometimes

makes men mad, it sometimes makes them great. Perhaps it makes them mad when their desire for it is intemperate, when they seek it for its own sake, not realizing that it must always be a given thing. The saints advise young mystics never to seek it. But young poets have no advisers with disciplinary power over them and they are more venturesome than religious neophytes. Having tasted the headiest wine of life they would be always drinking. Only the strongest wait until the draught is poured and know how to keep the chalice clean.

Much that is called ecstasy is not true ecstasy at all, but mere excitation. If there be no inhalation from power, love, truth, or beauty, then there can be no exhalation of them, no inspiration, no superb expression. Excitation can never produce more than a poor little gusty hiccup of a poem that is the result of spiritual indigestion, for which one should ask pardon.

Ecstasy can never be produced by a wind machine in a beauty parlor. It comes only from the primeval wind that bloweth where it listeth. It is always an element in the life of a genuine poet. It is the direct and certain result of his vitality and his sincerity. The excess of intellectual, emotional and spiritual vitality in him which leads him to seek expression in poetry, which makes him one with taut joys and agonies, brings him to his hour of ecstasy and of ecstatic utterance when he is ready for it, made ready by all of his preceding experience. The austere sincerity in him which makes it impossible for him to veil his darkest emotions from himself, makes him sure beyond self-questioning when he has found that ecstasy which is, as Yeats says, "a revelation of reality."

But because the most vital spiritual experience is likely to be misunderstood or mistaken for abstract thought or vaporous imagining by people who have, as yet, no clue to it in their own inner lives, I would refer the reader to that warm, rich, wise, beautiful book, "The Candle of Vision," by A. E., for a finer exposition of these things than I am able to give.

A POET'S PRAYER

That I have felt the rushing wind of Thee:
That I have run before Thy blast to sea;
That my one moment of transcendent strife
Is more than many years of listless life;
Beautiful Power, I praise Thee: yet I send
A prayer that sudden strength be not the end.
Desert me not when from my flagging sails
Thy breathing dies away, and virtue fails:
When Thou hast spent the glory of that gust,
Remember still the body of this dust.
Not then when I am boundless, without bars,
When I am rapt in hurry to the stars;
When I anticipate an endless bliss,
And feel before my time the final kiss,
Not then I need Thee: for delight is wise,
I err not in the freedom of the skies;
I fear not joy, so joy might ever be,
And rapture finish in felicity.
But when Thy joy is past; comes in the test,
To front the life that lingers after zest:
To live in mere negation of Thy light,

A more than blindness after more than sight.
'Tis not in flesh so swiftly to descend,
And sudden from the spheres with earth to blend;
And I, from splendour thrown, and dashed from dream,
Into the flare pursue the former gleam.
Sustain me in that hour with Thy left hand,
And aid me, when I cease to soar, to stand;
Make me Thy athlete even in my bed,
Thy girded runner though the course be sped;
Still to refrain that I may more bestow,
From sternness to a larger sweetness grow.
I ask not that false calm which many feign,
And call that peace which is a dearth of pain.
True calm doth quiver like the calmest star;
It is that white where all the colours are;
And for its very vestibule doth own
The tree of Jesus and the pyre of Joan.
Thither I press: but O do Thou meanwhile
Support me in privations of Thy smile.
Spaces Thou hast ordained the stars between
And silences where melody hath been:
Teach me those absences of fire to face,
And Thee no less in silence to embrace,
Else shall Thy dreadful gift still people Hell,
And men not measure from what height I fell.

—*Stephen Phillips*

From "Biographia Literaria."

The imagination then I consider either **as primary,** or
secondary. The primary imagination I hold to be the

living power and prime agent of all human perception, and as a repetition in the finite mind of the eternal act of creation in the infinite I AM. The secondary imagination I consider as an echo of the former, co-existing with the conscious will, yet still as identical with the primary in the *kind* of its agency, and differing only in degree, and in the mode of its operation. It dissolves, diffuses, dissipates, in order to re-create: or where this process is rendered impossible, yet still at all events it struggles to idealize and to unify. It is essentially *vital*, even as all objects (*as* objects) are essentially fixed and dead.

Fancy, on the contrary, has no other counters to play with, but fixities and definites. The fancy is indeed no other than a mode of memory emancipated from the order of time and space; while it is blended with and modified by that empirical phenomenon of the will which we express by the word "choice." But equally with the ordinary memory the fancy must receive all its materials ready made from the law of association.

—*Samuel Taylor Coleridge*

From a letter of Coleridge.

I never find myself alone, within the embracement of rocks and hills, . . . but my spirit careers, drives and eddies, like a leaf in autumn; a wild activity of thoughts, imaginations, feelings and impulses of motion rises up within me. . . . The further I ascend from animated nature . . . the greater in me becomes the intensity of the feeling of life. Life seems to me then an universal spirit, that neither has nor can have an opposite! God is everywhere, and where is there room for death?

—*Samuel Taylor Coleridge*

From "The Poet."

The universal nature, too strong for the petty nature of the bard, sits on his neck and writes through his hand; so that when he seems to vent a mere caprice and wild romance, the issue is an exact allegory. Hence Plato said that "poets utter great and wise things which they do not themselves understand." It is a secret which every intellectual man quickly learns, that beyond the energy of his possessed and conscious intellect he is capable of a new energy (as of an intellect doubled on itself), by abandonment to the nature of things; that, besides his privacy of power as an individual man, there is a great public power on which he can draw, by unlocking, at all risks, his human doors, and suffering the ethereal tides to roll and circulate through him: then he is caught up into the life of the Universe, his speech is thunder, his thought is law, and his words are universally intelligible as the plants and animals. The poet knows that he speaks adequately, then, only when he speaks somewhat wildly, or "with the flower of the mind"; not with the intellect used as an organ, but with the intellect released from all service, and suffered to take its direction from its celestial life; or, as the ancients were wont to express themselves, not with intellect alone, but with the intellect inebriated by nectar. As the traveler who has lost his way throws his reins on his horse's neck, and trusts to the instincts of the animal to

find his road, so must we do with the divine animal who
carries us through this world. For if in any manner we
can stimulate this instinct, new passages are opened for
us into nature, the mind flows into and through things
hardest and highest, and the metamorphosis is possible.

This is the reason why bards love wine, mead, narcotics,
coffee, tea, opium, the fumes of sandalwood and tobacco,
or whatever other species of animal exhilaration. All
men avail themselves of such means as they can, to add
this extraordinary power to their normal powers; and to
this end they prize conversation, music, pictures, sculpture, dancing, theaters, traveling, war, mobs, fires, gaming,
politics, or love, or science or animal intoxication which
are several coarser or finer *quasi*-mechanical substitutes
for the true nectar which is the ravishment of the intellect
by coming nearer to the fact. These are auxiliaries to
the centrifugal tendency of a man, to his passage out into
free space, and they help him to escape the custody of that
body in which he is pent up, and of that jail-yard of individual relations in which he is inclosed. Hence a great
number of such as were professionally expressors of Beauty,
as painters, poets, musicians and actors, have been more
than others wont to lead a life of pleasure and indulgence;
all but the few who received the true nectar; and, as
it was a spurious mode of attaining freedom, as it was an
emancipation not into the heavens, but into the freedom
of baser places, they were punished for that advantage they
won by a dissipation and deterioration. But never can
any advantage be taken of nature by a trick. The spirit
of the world, the great calm presence of the Creator,
comes not forth to the sorceries of opium or of wine. The

sublime vision comes to the pure and simple soul in a clean and chaste body. That is not an inspiration which we owe to narcotics, but some counterfeit excitement and fury.

—*Ralph Waldo Emerson*

What Anna Hempstead Branch thinks.

I believe that writing poetry is a process of listening. It is difficult to describe the state of delicate attention which alone makes it possible to hear and to remember that interior voice which sings, chants or speaks the poem. Where the voice comes from, whose it is, for what reason it comes and why it addresses itself to one's consciousness at that particular minute, are mysteries.

Sometimes it will sing an exuberant stanza in the midst of a funeral or a pensive ditty at a circus. At other times it lends itself to the emotion of the episode with exquisite adaptation. Sometimes it wreaths its music about a trivial event and makes its substance out of the glance of a wayfarer or the blowing of a curtain.

The voice is untamable, it is wilful, it is proud. It can be sought for with humility and occasionally the humility is rewarded. It likes better to come for Heavenly reasons of its own . . . and it is invariably lovely.

Sometimes its rapidity of utterance and its complexity of music make it impossible to capture. One hears many enchanting fragments of which one never hears the whole. The voice may begin at any time, no matter what one is doing. It may be singing the gentlest of music but it insists on its own way. It is not good for one to disregard it—unless one can transmute it into prayer or loveliness of action. If one speaks sharply or feels harshly or allows wrong thinking, the voice goes away, and in my own experience it seldom, under these circumstances, returns.

Many a temptation overcome creates a noble song and I suspect if we better understood the fine organisms of these living creatures—our poems—we would perceive that many a poem is in itself a fight. I doubt whether it is possible to define the many moods in which poems come. One can hear a poem almost anywhere if mental conditions are right, but it is easy to lose them and difficult to keep one's self long attuned to their music unless one has quiet hours for attention. The voice will wake one up in the middle of the night or begin its musical reverie in the midst of a conversation. I composed almost all of "The Warrior Maid" while I was engaged in a conversation with a friend. I was able to remember it afterwards and wrote it down. As little Samuel responded to the great Jehovah, so also must the poet answer, "Lord, here am I."

The first line arrives with a definite demand upon the attention. The others follow it. The first line decrees the music and the manner. I cannot change it. One does not recast a poem, after it begins to come, into another metre.

Some poems come with a magnetic aura of musical vibration in which I seem to be envelopt for several feet around. Sometimes I hear the music within for days before the words begin to come. Occasionally a poem brings with it a great sense of awe and the impact of tremendous vibrations. "Nimrod" and "The Marriage Feast" and

"It Took Me Ten Days to Read the Bible Through" all began with vision as well as music.

—*Anna Hempstead Branch*

From "The Candle of Vision."

I have failed in my purpose if I have not made it clear that in the actual architecture of dream and vision there is a mystery which is not explained by speaking of suppressed desire or sex or any of those springs which modern psychologists surmise are released in dream. A mood may attract its affinities but it does not create what it attracts, and between anger and a definite vision of conflict there is a gulf as mysterious as there was between Aladdin's desire and the building of his marvellous palace. I desire a house, but desire does not build it. I design a house, but every line is drawn with full consciousness, and when I give the plan to the builder every brick is placed with full consciousness by the masons. No coherent architecture in city or dream arises magically by some unreason which translates bodiless desire into organic form. However swift the succession may be, in that second of time between desire and its visionary embodiment or fulfilment there must be space for intellectual labour, the construction of forms or the choice of forms, and the endowing of them with motion. A second to my brain is too brief a fragment of time for more than sight, but I must believe that to a more intense consciousness, which is co-worker with mine, that second may suffice for a glimpse into some pleroma of form for the selection of these and the unrolling of a vast pageantry. Something there is, a creature within me, behind whose swiftness I falter a hopeless laggard, for it may be a traveller through the Archaeus and back again with the merchandise of its travel before my pulse has beaten twice. As an artist who has laboured slowly at the creation of pictures I assert that the forms of dream or vision if self-created require a conscious artist to arrange them, a magician to endow them with life, and that the process is intellectual, that is, it is conscious on some plane of being, though that self which sits in the gate of the body does not know what powers or dignitaries meet in the inner palace chambers of the soul. When we have dreams of flying and see all things from an angle of vision of which we never could have experience in waking, we know that to speak of the moving pictures of dream as memories or unconscious recombinations of things seen when waking, is to speak without subtlety or intellectual comprehension. I criticise the figures I see in dream or vision exactly as I would the figures in a painting. Even if I see a figure in dream I have seen when waking, if the figure acts in a manner differing from its action when seen with the physical eye, if it now walks when it then sat, or looks down where before it looked up, and if these motions in dream appear authentic so that face and form have the proper light and shade and the anatomies are undistorted, that dream change in the figure of memory is itself a most perplexing thing. We must suppose that memory as memory is as fixed in its way as a sunpicture is fixed or as the attitude of a statue is fixed. If it fades it should be by loss of precision and not into other equally precise but different forms and gestures. Now we could not without cracks or distorting of anatomies or complete remodelling change the pose of a statue even if it was modelled in some easily malleable substance; and the plastic change from stillness to motion in a figure, which we presume to be a memory, is wonderful when we think of it, as wonderful as if the little Tanagra in clay upon my shelf should change from its cast solidity and walk up and down before me. For myself I think man is a protean being, within whose unity there is diversity, and there are creatures in the soul which can inform the images of our memory, or the eternal memory, aye, and speak through them to us in dreams, so that we hear their voices, and it is with us in our minute microcosmic fashion even as it was said of the universe that it is a soliloquy of Deity wherein Ain-Soph talks to Ain-Soph.

—*A. E. (George Russell)*

From "The Candle of Vision."

I believed then, and still believe, that the immortal in us has memory of all its wisdom, or, as Keats puts it in one of his letters, there is an ancestral wisdom in man and we can if we wish drink that old wine of heaven. This memory of the spirit is the real basis of imagination, and when it speaks to us we feel truly inspired and a mightier creature than ourselves speaks through us. I remember how pure, holy and beautiful these imaginations seemed, how they came like crystal water sweeping aside the muddy current of my life, and the astonishment I felt, I who was almost inarticulate, to find sentences which seemed noble and full of melody sounding in my brain as if another and greater than I had spoken them; and how strange it was also a little later to write without effort verse, which some people still think has beauty, while I could hardly, because my reason had then no mastery over the materials of thought, pen a prose sentence intelligently. I am convinced that all poetry is, as Emerson said, first written in the heavens, that is, it is conceived by a self deeper than appears in normal life, and when it speaks to us or tells us its ancient story we taste of eternity and drink the Soma juice, the elixir of immortality.

—*A. E. (George Russell)*

From "Collected Poems."

When I first discovered for myself how near was the King in His beauty I thought I would be the singer of the happiest songs. Forgive me, Spirit of my spirit, for this, that I have found it easier to read the mystery told in tears and have understood Thee better in sorrow than in joy; that, though I would not, I have made the way seem thorny, and have wandered in too many by-ways, imagining myself into moods which held Thee not. I should have parted the true from the false, but I have not yet passed away from myself who am in the words of this book. Time is a swift winnower, and that he will do quickly for me.

—*A. E. (George Russell)*

INSPIRATION

Lightest of dancers, with no thought
Thy glimmering feet beat on my heart,
Gayest of singers, with no care
Waking to beauty the still air,
More than the labors of our art,
More than our wisdom can impart,
Thine idle ecstasy hath taught.

Lost long in solemn ponderings,
With the blind shepherd mind for guide,
The uncreated joy in you
Hath lifted up my heart unto
The morning stars in their first pride,
And the angelic joys that glide
High upon heaven-uplifted wings.

—*A. E. (George Russell)*

From Mark Pattison's "Life of Milton," Pamphlet 4.

None hath by more studious ways endeavoured, and with more unwearied spirit none shall—that I dare almost aver of myself, as far as life and full license will extend. Neither do I think it shame to covenant with any knowing reader that for some few years yet I may go on trust with him toward the payment of what I am now indebted, as being a work not to be raised from the heat of youth, or the vapours of wine, like that which flows at waste from the pen of some vulgar amorist, or the trencher fury of a rhyming parasite, nor to be obtained by the invocation of Dame Memory and her siren daughters, but by devout prayer to that Eternal Spirit who can enrich with all utterance and knowledge, and sends out his seraphim with the hallowed fire of his altar to touch and purify the life of whom he pleases. To this must be added industrious and select reading, steady observation, insight into all seemly and generous acts and affairs. Till which in some measure be compassed, at mine own peril and cost, I refuse not to sustain this expectation, from as many as are not loth to hazard so much credulity upon the best pledges that I can give them.

—*John Milton*

From "Introduction to the Works of Milton," by Corson. John Milton to Charles Diodati.

. . . Festivity and poetry are surely not incompatible. . . . One sees the triple influence of Bacchus, Apollo and Ceres, in the verses you have sent me. And, then, have you not music—the harp lightly touched by nimble hands, and the lute giving time to the fair ones as they dance in the old tapestried room? Believe me, where the ivory keys leap, and the accompanying dance goes round the perfumed hall, there will the Song-god be. But let me not go too far. Light Elegy is the care of many gods, and calls any one of them by turns to her assistance—Bacchus, Erato, Ceres, Venus, and little Cupid besides. To poets of this order, therefore, conviviality is allowable; and they may often indulge in draughts of good old wine. *But the man who speaks of high matters—the heaven of the full-grown Jove, and pious heroes, and demi-god leaders of*

*men, the man who now sings the holy counsels of the gods
above, and now the subterranean realms guarded by the
fierce dog—let him live sparely, after the manner of the
Samian master; let herbs afford him his innocent diet, let
clear water in a beechen cup stand near him, and let him
drink sober draughts from a pure fountain! To this be
there added a youth chaste and free from guilt, and rigid
morals, and hands without stain. Being such, thou shalt
rise up, glittering in sacred raiment and purified by lustral
waters, an augur about to go into the presence of the
unoffended gods.* So is wise Tiresias said to have lived,
after he had been deprived of his sight; and Theban Linus;
and Calchas the exile; and old Orpheus. So did the
scantily-eating, water-drinking Homer carry his hero
Ulysses through the monster-teeming hall of Circe, and
the straits insidious with the voices of the Syrens, and
through thy courts, too, O infernal King, where he is said
to have held the troops of shades enthralled by libations of
black blood. For the poet is sacred and the priest of the
gods; and his breast and his mouth breathe the indwelling
Jove.

And now, if you will know what I am myself doing (if
indeed you think it is of so much consequence to know
if I am doing anything), here is the fact: we are engaged
in singing the heavenly birth of the King of Peace, and
the happy age promised by the holy books, and the infant
cries and cradling in a manger under a poor roof of that
God who rules, with his Father, the Kingdom of Heaven,
and the sky with the new-sprung star in it, and the ethereal
choirs of hymning angels, and the gods of the heathen
suddenly fleeing to their endangered fanes. This is the

gift which we have presented to Christ's natal day. On that very morning, at daybreak, it was first conceived. The verses, which are composed in the vernacular, await you in close keeping; you shall be the judge to whom I shall recite them.

—*John Milton*

From "Milton's Works"—Areopagitica.

For Books are not absolutely dead things, but doe contain a potencie of Life in them to be as active as that Soule was whose progeny they are; nay they doe preserve as in a violl the purest efficacie and extraction of that living intellect that bred them. I know they are as lively, and as vigorously productive, as those fabulous Dragon's teeth; and being sown up and down, may chance to spring up armed men. And yet on the other hand unlesse warinesse be us'd, as good almost kill a Man as kill a good Book; who kills a Man kills a reasonable creature, God's Image; but hee who destroys a good Booke, kills reason it selfe, kills the Image of God, as it were in the eye. Many a man lives a burden to the Earth; but a good Booke is the pretious life-blood of a master spirit imbalm'd and treasur'd up on purpose to a life beyond life.

—*John Milton*

From "The Letters of William Blake." To Butts, concerning the "Milton."

. . . But, alas! now I may say to you—what perhaps I should not dare to say to anyone else: that I can alone

carry on my visionary studies in London unannoyed, and
that I may converse with my friends in eternity, see visions,
dream dreams, and prophesy and speak parables unob-
served, and at liberty from the doubts of other mortals;
perhaps doubts proceeding from kindness; but doubts are
always pernicious, especially when we doubt our friends.
Christ is very decided on this point: "He who is not
with Me is against Me." There is no medium or middle
state; and if a man is the enemy of my spiritual life while
he pretends to be the friend of my corporeal, he is a real
enemy; but the man may be the friend of my spiritual life
while he seems the enemy of my corporeal, though not
vice versa.

What is very pleasant, every one who hears of my going
to London again applauds it as the only course for the
interest of all concerned in my works; observing that I
ought not to be away from the opportunities London affords of seeing fine pictures, and the various improve-
ments in works of art going on in London.

But none can know the spiritual acts of my three years'
slumber on the banks of ocean, unless he has seen them in
the spirit, or unless he should read my long poem descriptive of those acts; for I have in these years composed an
immense number of verses on one grand theme, similar
to Homer's *Iliad* or Milton's *Paradise Lost;* the persons
and machinery entirely new to the inhabitants of earth
(some of the persons excepted). I have written this poem
from immediate dictation, twelve or sometimes twenty or
thirty lines at a time, without premeditation, and even
against my will. The time it has taken in writing was
thus rendered non-existent, and an immense poem exists

which seems to be the labour of a long life, all produced without labour or study. I mention this to show you what I think the grand reason of my being brought down here.

I have a thousand and ten thousand things to say to you. My heart is full of futurity. I perceive that the sore travail which has been given me these three years leads to glory and honour. I rejoice and tremble: "I am fearfully and wonderfully made." I had been reading the cxxxix Psalm a little before your letter arrived. I take your advice. I see the face of my Heavenly Father. He lays His hand upon my head, and gives a blessing to all my work. Why should I be troubled? Why should my heart and flesh cry out? I will go on in the strength of the Lord; through Hell will I sing forth His praises; that the dragons of the deep may praise Him, and that those who dwell in darkness and in the sea coasts may be gathered into His kingdom. Excuse my, perhaps, too great enthusiasm.

—*William Blake*

From "The Letters of William Blake." Letter to Butts.

. . . The thing I have most at heart—more than life, or all that seems to make life comfortable . . . is the interest of true religion and science. And whenever anything appears to affect that interest (especially if I myself omit any duty to my station as a soldier of Christ), it gives me the greatest of torments. I am not ashamed, afraid, or averse to tell you what ought to be told: that I am under the direction of messengers from heaven, daily and nightly.

But the nature of such things is not, as some suppose, without trouble or care. Temptations are on the right hand and on the left. Behind, the sea of time and space roars and follows swiftly. He who keeps not right onwards is lost; and if our footsteps slide in clay, how can we do otherwise than fear and tremble? But I should not have troubled you with this account of my spiritual state, unless it had been necessary in explaining the actual cause of my uneasiness, into which you are so kind as to inquire; for I never obtrude such things on others unless questioned, and then I never disguise the truth. But if we fear to do the dictates of our angels, and tremble at the tasks set before us; if we refuse to do spiritual acts because of natural fears or natural desires, who can describe the dismal torments of such a state! I too well remember the threats I heard!—"If you, who are organised by Divine Providence for spiritual communion, refuse, and bury your talent in the earth, even though you should want natural bread, sorrow and desperation pursue you through life, and after death shame and confusion of face to eternity. Everyone in eternity will leave you, aghast at the man who was crowned with glory and honour by his brethren, and betrayed their cause to their enemies. You will be called the base Judas who betrayed his friend!" Such words would make any stout man tremble, and how then could I be at ease? But I am now no longer in that state, and now go on again with my task, fearless, though my path is difficult. I have no fear of stumbling while I keep it.

—*William Blake*

HYMN TO INTELLECTUAL BEAUTY

I

The awful shadow of some unseen Power
  Floats though unseen among us,—visiting
  This various world with as inconstant wing
As summer winds that creep from flower to flower,—
Like moonbeams that behind some piny mountain
    shower,
  It visits with inconstant glance
  Each human heart and countenance;
Like hues and harmonies of evening,—
  Like clouds in starlight widely spread,—
  Like memory of music fled,—
  Like aught that for its grace may be
Dear, and yet dearer for its mystery.

II

Spirit of BEAUTY, that dost consecrate
  With thine own hues all thou dost shine upon
  Of human thought or form,—where art thou gone?
Why dost thou pass away and leave our state,
This dim vast vale of tears, vacant and desolate?
  Ask why the sunlight not for ever
  Weaves rainbows o'er yon mountain-river,
Why aught should fail and fade that once is shown,
  Why fear and dream and death and birth
  Cast on the daylight of this earth
  Such gloom,—why man has such a scope
For love and hate, despondency and hope?

III

No voice from some sublimer world hath ever
  To sage or poet these responses given—
  Therefore the names of Demon, Ghost, and Heaven.
Remain the records of their vain endeavour,
Frail spells—whose uttered charm might not avail to
      sever,
  From all we hear and all we see,
  Doubt, chance, and mutability.
Thy light alone—like mist o'er mountains driven,
  Or music by the night-wind sent
  Through strings of some still instrument,
  Or moonlight on a midnight stream,
Gives grace and truth to life's unquiet dream.

IV

Love, Hope, and Self-esteem, like clouds depart
  And come, for some uncertain moments lent.
  Man were immortal, and omnipotent,
Didst thou, unknown and awful as thou art,
Keep with thy glorious train firm state within his
      heart.
  Thou messenger of sympathies,
  That wax and wane in lovers' eyes—
Thou—that to human thought art nourishment,
  Like darkness to a dying flame!
  Depart not as thy shadow came,
  Depart not—lest the grave should be,
Like life and fear, a dark reality.

V

While yet a boy I sought for ghosts, and sped
  Through many a listening chamber, cave and ruin,
  And starlight wood, with fearful steps pursuing
Hopes of high talk with the departed dead.
I called on poisonous names with which our youth is
    fed;
  I was not heard—I saw them not—
  When musing deeply on the lot
Of life, at that sweet time when winds are wooing
  All vital things that wake to bring
  News of birds and blossoming,—
  Sudden, thy shadow fell on me;
I shrieked, and clasped my hands in ecstasy!

VI

I vowed that I would dedicate my powers
  To thee and thine—have I not kept the vow?
  With beating heart and streaming eyes, even now
I call the phantoms of a thousand hours
Each from his voiceless grave; they have in visioned
    bowers
  Of studious zeal or love's delight
  Outwatched with me the envious night—
They know that never joy illumed my brow
  Unlinked with hope that thou wouldst free
  This world from its dark slavery,
  That thou—O awful LOVELINESS,
Wouldst give whate'er these words cannot express.

VII

The day becomes more solemn and serene
  When noon is past—there is a harmony
  In autumn, and a lustre in its sky,
Which through the summer is not heard or seen,
As if it could not be, as if it had not been!
    Thus let thy power, which like the truth
    Of nature on my passive youth
  Descended, to my onward life supply
    Its calm—to one who worships thee,
    And every form containing thee,
    Whom, SPIRIT fair, thy spells did bind
  To fear himself, and love all human kind.

From "Letters of Percy Bysshe Shelley," by Ingpen.   To Leigh Hunt.

Next will I own the "Hymn to Intellectual Beauty"? I do not care—as you like. And yet the poem was composed under the influence of feelings which agitated me even to tears, so that I think it deserves a better fate than the being linked with so stigmatised and unpopular a name (so far as it is known) as mine. You will say that it is not thus, that I am morbidly sensitive to what I esteem the injustice of neglect—but I do not say that I am unjustly neglected, the oblivion which overtook my little attempt of "Alastor" I am ready to acknowledge was sufficiently merited in *itself*: but then it was not accorded in the correct proportion considering the success of the most contemptible drivellings. I am undeceived in the belief that I have powers deeply to interest, or sub-

stantially to improve, mankind. How far my conduct and
my opinions have rendered the zeal and ardour with which
I have engaged in the attempt ineffectual, I know not. Self
love prompts me to assign much weight to a cause which
perhaps has none. But this much I do not seek to conceal
from myself, that I am an outcast from human society;
my name is execrated by all who understand its entire import—by those very beings whose happiness I ardently
desire.

—Percy Bysshe Shelley

From "Interpretations of Poetry and Religion."

Religion is poetry become the guide of life, poetry sub-
stituted for science or supervening upon it as an approach
to the highest reality. Poetry is religion allowed to drift,
left without points of application in conduct and without
an expression in worship and dogma: it is religion without practical efficacy and without metaphysical illusion.
The ground of this abstractness of poetry, however, is
usually only its narrow scope: a poet who plays with an
idea for half an hour, or constructs a character to which
he gives no profound moral significance, forgets his own
thought, or remembers it only as a fiction of his leisure,
because he has not dug his well deep enough to tap the
subterranean springs of his own life. But when the poet
enlarges his theatre and puts into his rhapsodies the true
visions of his people and of his soul, his poetry is the con-
secration of his deepest convictions, and contains the whole
truth of his religion. What the religion of the vulgar

adds to the poet's is simply the inertia of their limited apprehension, which takes literally what he meant ideally, and degrades into a false extension of this world on its own level what in his mind was a true interpretation of it upon a moral plane.

—*George Santayana*

From "The Necessity of Poetry."

As to the relation of Poetry to religion. True Religion, the conviction and habit of a personal communion between the soul and God, is of too unique and jealous a temper to allow of any artistic predominance: and yet we find the best expression of it in Poetry: indeed the poetic expression of the spiritual life is of such force that its beauty may hold the mind in slavery to false ideals.

I believe it to be greatly due to this that the English people are still mentally enslaved to a conception of God altogether unworthy and incompatible with our better notions: and, if it is the old Hebrew poetry which is greatly responsible for this delusion, then it seems reasonable to look to our own poets for our release.

On this general question of religion I shall take only that one point. We have spiritually outgrown the theology of the Reformation, and our churches, in endeavouring to make their obsolete ideals work, find their most effective agent in the beauty of our English translation of the Old Testament which, while secular art was in decay, captured the artistic susceptibility of the people.

—*Robert Bridges*

SONG FOR ST. CECILIA'S DAY, 1687

From Harmony, from heavenly Harmony
   This universal frame began:
  When Nature underneath a heap
   Of jarring atoms lay
 And could not heave her head,
The tuneful voice was heard from high,
   Arise, ye more than dead!
Then cold and hot and moist and dry
In order to their stations leap,
  And Music's power obey.
From Harmony, from heavenly Harmony
   This universal frame began:
  From harmony to harmony
Through all the compass of the notes it ran,
The diapason closing full in Man.

What passion cannot Music raise and quell?
   When Jubal struck the chorded shell
  His listening brethren stood around,
  And, wondering, on their faces fell
  To worship that celestial sound.
Less than a god they thought there could not dwell
   Within the hollow of that shell
   That spoke so sweetly and so well.
What passion cannot Music raise and quell?

  The trumpet's loud clangor
   Excites us to arms,
  With shrill notes of anger
   And mortal alarms.

The double double double beat
   Of the thundering drum
   Cries "Hark! the foes come;
Charge, charge, 'tis too late to retreat!"

The soft complaining flute
   In dying notes discovers
   The woes of hopeless lovers,
Whose dirge is whisper'd by the warbling lute.

Sharp violins proclaim
Their jealous pangs and desperation,
Fury, frantic indignation,
Depth of pains, and height of passion
   For the fair disdainful dame.

But oh! what art can teach,
What human voice can reach
   The sacred organ's praise?
Notes inspiring holy love,
Notes that wing their heavenly ways
   To mend the choirs above.

Orpheus could lead the savage race,
And trees unrooted left their place
   Sequacious of the lyre:
But bright Cecilia raised the wonder higher:
When to her Organ vocal breath was given
An Angel heard, and straight appear'd—
   Mistaking Earth for Heaven.

Grand Chorus

As from the power of sacred lays
   The spheres began to move,
And sung the great Creator's praise
   To all the blest above;
So when the last and dreadful hour
This crumbling pageant shall devour,
The trumpet shall be heard on high,
The dead shall live, the living die,
And music shall untune the sky.

—John Dryden

From "Per Amica Silentia Lunae."

We make out of the quarrel with others, rhetoric, but of the quarrel with ourselves, poetry. Unlike the rhetoricians, who get a confident voice from remembering the crowd they have won or may win, we sing amid our uncertainty; and, smitten even in the presence of the most high beauty by the knowledge of our solitude, our rhythm shudders. I think, too, that no fine poet, no matter how disordered his life, has ever, even in his mere life, had pleasure for his end. Johnson and Dowson, friends of my youth, were dissipated men, the one a drunkard, the other a drunkard and mad about women, and yet they had the gravity of men who had found life out and were awakening from the dream; and both, one in life and art and one in art and less in life, had a continual preoccupation with religion. Nor has any poet I have read of or heard of or met with been a sentimentalist. The other self, the anti-self or the antithetical self, as one may choose to name it, comes but to those who are no longer deceived,

whose passion is reality. The sentimentalists are practical men who believe in money, in position, in a marriage
bell, and whose understanding of happiness is to be so busy
whether at work or at play, that all is forgotten but the
momentary aim. They find their pleasure in a cup that
is filled from Lethe's wharf, and for the awakening, for
the vision, for the revelation of reality, tradition offers us
a different word—ecstasy. An old artist wrote to me of
his wanderings by the quays of New York, and how he
found there a woman nursing a sick child, and drew her
story from her. She spoke, too, of other children who had
died: a long tragic story. "I wanted to paint her," he
wrote, "if I denied myself any of the pain I could not
believe in my own ecstasy." We must not make a false
faith by hiding from our thoughts the causes of doubt, for
faith is the highest achievement of the human intellect,
the only gift man can make to God, and therefore it must
be offered in sincerity. Neither must we create, by hiding
ugliness, a false beauty as our offering to the world. He
only can create the greatest imaginable beauty who has
endured all imaginable pangs, for only when we have seen
and foreseen what we dread shall we be rewarded by
that dazzling unforeseen wing-footed wanderer.

—*William Butler Yeats*

From "Inspiration."

Something—they know not what—but something greater
than the man speaks through the man, and there is a virtue
in his works that his own unaided power never placed there.
I think I describe the feeling fairly in these words. Inspiration is a natural conviction of men with respect to

poetry; and to the greater poets themselves it is as natural, for their own works and their states of mind in composing seem beyond and above themselves. This sense of possession, of being caught up into a sphere of greater power, is the true poetic madness, which is so familiar an idea in Greek thought, and is not yet extinct.

I have a theory—whether I have read it or dreamed it I do not know—that the emergence of man from the brute-stage of life was accompanied by an immense outburst and increase of emotional power. If it were so, the emotion was of this kind; and, without regard to the scientific ground of the theory, it appears to me *prima facie* plausible to this degree, that such emotion was a main condition of the gradual advent of intellectual life. If we remember how weak and unstable then were all mental phenomena, still perhaps more like waking dreams than what we know as continuous and organized mental life, and if we remember also the power of emotion to vivify the mental processes, it is plain that minds so stirred would grow and would store power beyond other minds. The phenomenon would be only what is our well-known experience taking place in a lower plane of being. Excitement increases the speed and power of the mind; the use of stimulants affords such excitement, and when the excitement arises naturally through the emotions, the effect is the same. The state so induced, whether naturally or artificially, does not differ in kind from that of inspiration—that is, a power above the normal from which the subject of it recedes when the mood is gone.

—*George Edward Woodberry*

Let poetry once more be restored to her ancient truth and purity; let her be inspired from heaven, and, in return, her incense ascend thither; let her exchange her low, venal, trifling subjects for such as are fair, useful, and magnificent: and let her execute these so as at once to please, instruct, surprise, and astonish; and then, of necessity, the most inveterate ignorance and prejudice shall be struck dumb, and poets yet become the delight and wonder of mankind.

—*James Thomson* (1700-1748)

From "Sordello."

How a poet's soul comes into play.

How can such love?—like souls on each full-fraught
Discovery brooding, blind at first to aught
Beyond its beauty, till exceeding love
Becomes an aching weight; and, to remove
A curse that haunts such natures—to preclude
Their finding out themselves can work no good
To what they love nor make it very blest
By their endeavor,—they are fain invest
The lifeless thing with life from their own soul,
Availing it to purpose, to control,
To dwell distinct and have peculiar joy
And separate interests that may employ
That beauty fitly, for its proper sake.
Nor rest they here; fresh births of beauty wake
Fresh homage, every grade of love is past,
With every mode of loveliness: then cast
Inferior idols off their borrowed crown

Before a coming glory. Up and down
Runs arrowy fire, while earthly forms combine
To throb the secret forth; a touch divine—
And the scaled eyeball owns the mystic rod;
Visibly through his garden walketh God.

—*Robert Browning*

From "The Prelude."

    Wisdom and Spirit of the Universe!
Thou Soul that art the eternity of thought
That givest to forms and images a breath
And everlasting motion, not in vain
By day or star-light thus from my first dawn
Of childhood didst thou intertwine for me
The passions that build up our human soul;
Not with the mean and vulgar works of man,
But with high objects, with enduring things—
With life and nature—purifying thus
The elements of feeling and of thought,
And sanctifying, by such discipline,
Both pain and fear, until we recognise
A grandeur in the beatings of the heart.

—*William Wordsworth*

OCTOBER

AEGLOGA DECIMA

ARGUMENT

In Cuddie is set out the perfecte paterne of a poete,
whiche, finding no maintenaunce of his state and studies,

complayneth of the contempte of Poetrie, and the causes
thereof: specially having bene in all ages, and even amongst
the most barbarous, alwayes of singular accounpt and
honor, and being indede so worthy and commendable an
arte: or rather no arte, but a divine gift and heavenly
instinct, not to bee gotten by laboure and learning, but
adorned with both, and poured into the witte by a certain
ἐνθουσιασμός and celestiall inspiration; as the author hereof
else where at large discourseth in his booke called *The
English Poete*, which booke being lately come to my hands,
I mynde also by God's grace, upon further advisement,
to publish.

PIERCE. CUDDIE.

Piers. Cuddie, for shame! hold up thy heavye head,
And let us cast with what delight to chace
And weary thys long lingring Phœbus race.
Whilome thou wont the shepheards laddes to leade
In rymes, in ridles, and in bydding base:
Now they in thee, and thou in sleepe art dead.

Cud. Piers, I have pyped erst so long with payne,
That all mine oten reedes bene rent and wore:
And my poore Muse hath spent her spared store,
Yet little good hath got, and much lesse gayne.
Such pleasaunce makes the grashopper so poore,
And ligge so layd, when winter doth her straine.

The dapper ditties that I wont devise,
To feede youthes fancie and the flocking fry,
Delighten much: what I the bett forthy?

They han the pleasure, I a sclender prise:
I beate the bush, the byrds to them doe flye:
What good thereof to Cuddie can arise?

Piers. Cuddie, the prayse is better then the price,
The glory eke much greater then the gayne
O what an honor is it, to restraine
The lust of lawlesse youth with good advice,
Or pricke them forth with pleasaunce of thy vaine,
Whereto thou list their trayned willes entice!

Soone as thou gynst to sette thy notes in frame,
O how the rurall routes to thee doe cleave!
Seemeth thou doest their soule of sense bereave,
All as the shepheard, that did fetch his dame
From Plutoes balefull bowre withouten leave:
His musicks might the hellish hound did tame.

Cud. So praysen babes the peacoks spotted traine,
And wondren at bright Argus blazing eye;
But who rewards him ere the more forthy?
Or feedes him once the fuller by a graine?
Sike prayse is smoke, that sheddeth in the skye,
Sike words bene wynd, and wasten soone in vayne.

Piers. Abandon then the base and viler clowne:
Lyft up thy selfe out of the lowly dust,
And sing of bloody Mars, of wars, of giusts:
Turne thee to those that weld the awful crowne,
To doubted knights, whose woundlesse armour rusts,
And helmes unbruzed wexen dayly browne.

There may thy Muse display her fluttryng wing,
And stretch her selfe at large from east to west:
Whither thou list in fayre Elisa rest,
Or if thee please in bigger notes to sing,
Advaunce the worthy whome shee loveth best,
That first the white beare to the stake did bring.

And when the stubborne stroke of stronger stounds
Has somewhat slackt the tenor of thy string,
Of love and lustihead tho mayst thou sing,
And carrol lowde, and leade the myllers rownde,
All were Elisa one of thilke same ring.
So mought our Cuddies name to heaven sownde.

Cud. Indeede the Romish Tityrus, I heare,
Through his Mecœnas left his oaten reede,
Whereon he earst had taught his flocks to feede,
And laboured lands to yield the timely eare,
And eft did sing of warres and deadly drede,
So as the heavens did quake his verse to here.

But ah! Mecœnas is yclad in claye,
And great Augustus long ygoe is dead,
And all the worthies liggen wrapt in leade,
That matter made for poets on to play:
For, ever, who in derring doe were dreade,
The loftie verse of hem was loved aye.

But after vertue gan for age to stoupe,
And mighty manhode brought a bedde of ease,
The vaunting poets found nought worth a pease

To put in preace emong the learned troupe.
Tho gan the streames of flowing wittes to cease,
And sonnebright honour pend in shamefull coupe.

And if that any buddes of poesie
Yet of the old stocke gan to shoote agayne,
Or it mens follies mote be forst to fayne,
And rolle with rest in rymes of rybaudrye,
Or, as it sprong, it wither must agayne:
Tom Piper makes us better melodie.

Piers. O pierlesse Poesye, where is then thy place?
If nor in princes pallace thou doe sitt,
(And yet is princes pallace the most fitt)
Ne brest of baser birth doth thee embrace.
Then make thee winges of thine aspyring wit,
And, whence thou camst, flye backe to heaven apace.

Cud. Ah, Percy! it is all to weake and wanne,
So high to sore, and make so large a flight;
Her peeced pyneons bene not so in plight:
For Colin fittes such famous flight to scanne:
He, were he not with love so ill bedight,
Would mount as high and sing as soote as swanne.

Piers. Ah, fon! for love does teach him climbe so hie,
And lyftes him up out of the loathsome myre:
Such immortall mirrhor as he doth admire
Would rayse ones mynd above the starry skie,
And cause a caytive corage to aspire;
For lofty love doth loath a lowly eye.

Cud. All otherwise the state of poet stands:
For lordly Love is such a tyranne fell,
That, where he rules, all power he doth expell.
The vaunted verse a vacant head demaundes,
Ne wont with crabbed Care the Muses dwell:
Unwisely weaves, that takes two webbes in hand.

Who ever casts to compasse weightye prise,
And thinks to throwe out thondring words of threate,
Let powre in lavish cups and thriftie bitts of meate;
For Bacchus fruite is frend to Phœbus wise,
And when with wine the braine begins to sweate,
The nombers flowe as fast as spring doth ryse.

Thou kenst not, Percy, howe the ryme should rage.
O if my temples were distaind with wine,
And girt in girlonds of wild yvie twine,
How I could reare the Muse on stately stage,
And teache her tread aloft in buskin fine,
With queint Bellona in her equipage!

But ah! my corage cooles ere it be warme;
Forthy content us in thys humble shade,
Where no such troublous tydes han us assayde.
Here we our slender pipes may safely charme.
Piers. And when my gates shall han their bellies layd,
Cuddie shall have a kidde to store his farme.

EMBLEME

Hereby is meant, as also in the whole course of this
Æglogue, that poetry is a divine instinct and unnatural

rage passing the reache of comen reason. Whom Piers
answereth epiphonematicos, as admiring the excellency of
the skyll, whereof in Cuddie hee hadde alreadye hadde a
taste.

—*Edmund Spenser*

* PARACLETE

Tongue hath not told it,
    Heart hath not known;
Yet shall the bough swing
    When it hath flown.

Dreams have denied it,
    Fools forsworn:
Yet it hath comforted
    Each man born

Once and again it is
    Blown to me
Sweet from the wild thyme,
    Salt from the sea;

Blown thro' the ferns
    Faint from the sky;
Shadowed in water,
    Yet clear as a cry

Light on a face,
    Or touch of a hand,

* Reprinted by permission from "Collected Poems," Volume III,
by Alfred Noyes. Copyright, 1915, by Frederick A. Stokes Company.

Making my still heart
  Understand.

Earth has not seen it,
  Nor heaven above,
Yet shall the wild bough
  Bend with the Dove.

Yea, tho' the bloom fall
  Under Thy feet,
Veni, Creator,
  Paraclete!

—*Alfred Noyes*

NOT EVERY DAY FIT FOR VERSE

'Tis not ev'ry day, that I
Fitted am to prophesie:
No, but when the Spirit fils
The fantastick Pannicles:
Full of fier; then I write
As the Godhead doth indite.
Thus inrag'd, my lines are hurl'd,
Like the *Sybells,* through the world.
Look how next the holy fier
Either slakes, or doth retire;
So the Fancie cooles, till when
That brave Spirit comes agen.

—*Robert Herrick*

Singing is sweet; but be sure of this,
Lips only sing when they cannot kiss.

—*James Thomson* (1834-1882)

THE SECONDARY INSPIRATION

To explore the sources of poetic inspiration in any poet is to discover the governing power in that personality, the love that draws him as toward his own, or conversely, the hatred that fills him with zeal in the denunciation of all that is opposed to the thing beloved. Inspiration is like love rewarding desire. For whether a poet loves nature or a woman, sculpture or music, his spirit tends to be at one with the essence that he cares for; he takes upon his mind the stamp of the image of loveliness which he adores and gives back to it, when he tells of it in words, his own image and superscription. It is no mere metaphorical exaggeration to say that Wordsworth and Whitman were wedded to nature and Shelley to sculpture and other beauties. Even the inspiration which led Blake to believe that he could praise his own poems because they were dictated from Heaven, because their true authors were "in eternity," was the result of the almighty love of his soul for Almighty God.

This is true because love, and hatred, which is only the negative power of love—love with a minus sign—are the only forces that can induce the long contemplation without which true inspiration does not come. This contemplation may be unconscious brooding, a slow process carried on in the subconscious mind, or it may be a firm concentration of the will as it is with A. E. But it is always essential. Burns, forever ready to surrender his heart to the incursion of a woman's grace and beauty; Shelley, who could spend hours at a time gazing on a famous Apollo, or Minerva, or Niobe; Keats, who drank Shakespeare as a fish drinks the sea; Whitman, who in libraries was "dumb, a gawk, or unborn, or dead," who believed that all free poems are conceived in the open air; William Vaughn Moody, who burned with a passion against social injustice before he wrote "Gloucester Moors";—all these have fallen in love with that in life which could energize mind, heart, and spirit, preparing them for completest utterance. The poet is drawn by his desire, he perceives, loves, contemplates; then the essential union of qualities is consummated, power is generated, and truth and beauty are spoken. The nobler his desire is, the loftier perception, love, and contemplation are likely to be; the greater the power, also, and the more valuable the gift when it is given. For we and our works tend to become like our desires, or are conditioned by them. The thoughts of gods are divine, but, as Emerson wittily says, "the thoughts of turtles are turtles."

But let us notice carefully that it is not the fulfillment of any physical desire on the material plane of existence that is responsible for inspiration and makes it valid. The greatest poetry may come out of the agony of denial, out of the love that is pain. As Ridgely Torrence says,

> Love had pierced into my human sheathing,
> Song came out of me simple as breathing—

Indeed it almost seems, sometimes, as if the thwarting of the material fulfillment intensifies and deepens contemplation and thereby increases the value of the poet's gift. If Dante had won his Beatrice, would he have set her forever in a luminous Heaven? Whitman, who was no ascetic, said, "I loved a certain person ardently and my love was not return'd, yet out of that have I written these songs." It is not the incontinent desire that produces the finest work, but the emotion held in the mind so long and contemplated so steadfastly that it crystallizes into perfect images and symbols of the finest, clearest, and most vital thought. What the poet does not spend without restraint in his daily life he can express with glorious restraint as an artist.

This brings before us a theory of genius formulated by William Butler Yeats, the theory that genius is the triumph of an antithetical self over the actual and every-day self in the poet. To be thoroughly understood the theory must be discussed at length, but it is well to note here that he says Keats filled his poems with images of sensuous beauty because, in his boyhood, he was denied the pleasure of possessing and enjoying beautiful objects. It is worth while to mention, also, something that Robert Graves says truly and entertainingly in "On English Poetry," namely, that the poet who describes any particular theme of contemplation or inspiration to a friend has probably lost the chance of making it into a poem. It is spent in conversation. The coals are scattered and the red dies out of the embers. Other poets go so far as to believe that poetry itself, which comes out of profound reality, is often a substitution of the symbol for the actual, of words for life. The later James Thomson said,

Lips only sing when they cannot kiss.

These suggestions are pertinent and worthy of consideration at the present time because the idea is current in certain literary circles that a lack of personal poise is favorable to the creation of poetry, that the emotional spendthrift is usually and necessarily more of an artist than the quiet master who holds that he may give. The cry for ''experience'' is often the cry for relaxing experience. The penalty paid for relaxing experience is a lowering of the tone of thought and feeling. This very lowering of tone may bring a temporary popularity, for it is easier to meet mankind where they are than to lead them into austere uplands of the spirit. But the penalty of that popularity is inevitable deterioration. Little by little the poet's fire will burn more smokily. Perhaps even before the popularity is fairly won, the bowstring of his thought will be less taut and secure so that his arrows fall short of the quarry that should have been his. The spokesman for the emotional spendthrift should remember that experience is something which a live personality can hardly avoid. For the quick it is inevitable, and perhaps even the dead have enough of it and to spare. To a certain extent we are free agents and may choose between one kind of experience and another. But we cannot be strong and intense while we are flabby and slack, we cannot be going upstairs while we are coming down. We may also choose our own ways of interpreting experience. The great poet will use it grandly. As for folly, it may be dear and delicious—in retrospect—to everybody but the fool!

If I were asked to reconcile this theory of restraint with the lovable achievements of a poet like Burns whose affairs with women were many and untrammeled, I should say that I believe that the inspiration which he found in them, in so far as it was valid, was found in the love, not in the sexual expression of it. Love is always inspiring and it is better to love unworthily than never to love at all—if that be possible for a living creature. The world needs more human affection, not less, more even of the friendship of women for men, and of men for women. This, which is commonly a cause of fear, jealousy, and sorrow, should be, and could be were Christianity real among us, a great inspiring force not only in the arts, but in the common life. Looking far into the future toward a society that has learned finer self-control and the technique of stabilizing personalities in healthier sympathies, we may believe in friendships like that of St. Francis and Sta. Clara, and in others as sound and sensitive, though less exalted. And apropos of that, one of the most beautiful poems of the period, one of the noblest and most austere lyrics of love in the language, is Sarah N. Cleghorn's "Sta Clare Hears St. Francis" recently published in "The World To-morrow." The poet who seeks an affection merely that inspiration may result, let him be anathema; but the grand truth is that when we care for each other we seek something divine and often find it. That divinity is inspiration. The pitiful truth is that we have not yet learned how to separate that desire of divinity from the mere lust of possession in the minds of mankind, we have not been able to make mankind believe in it, and consequently we are still dominated by fears and suspicions. Only the long ages can teach us how to live together here on earth happily and poetically.

If we choose to ask ourselves how this inspiration that comes through the love of people or of nature or of great art differs from the inspiration that comes to a Blake or a Milton in response to prayer, we shall have to say, I think, that it differs only in being somewhat less direct. If the Holy Ghost is given at all to any poets, then He that spake by the prophets is the same that is apparent, though veiled and vaguely, to Burns in a woman's beauty. He drew near to Wordsworth in the open fields and talked to Shelley with lips of marble. Indeed, the author of "The Golden Bough" says that music can recreate for the hearer the primary religious inspiration which gave it birth, and he has interesting things to say of its use for that purpose among primitive peoples. But though this secondary inspiration, inspiration through various kinds of mediums, is as divine in origin as the primary inspiration by contact with God, it is less immediate. The wind of the world is tempered by that through which its breath is blown. The light of the world is shown in a spectrum.

It would be crude to suppose, however, that the man who is inspired by music must necessarily write his poems about it, or that gazing on statues make verses about statuary. Our minds and hearts are so complex, our thoughts and feelings so intricately woven together, that even an innocent daisy may be responsible for a poem about a jailbird. Poets are just as mysterious as other people when we come to consider the actions and reactions of their intellects.

We may ask ourselves, also, why it is that some days are fertile and others fruitless, why a poet may go for months without making so much as a quatrain out of his experience and then turn out three poems in a night as Meredith once did, or have what Pope called an "extraordinary flux of rhyme" of three days' duration. The poets have asked themselves this question, but have found no conclusive answer. There is no way of forcing union hours on poets, or making a poetry machine that will turn out poems by the yard. Donne says pithily,

> Like one who in her third widowhood doth profess
> Herself a nun, tied to retiredness,
> So affects my muse now a chaste fallowness.

Or, to quote a more wistful comment on the familiar fact, "The Muse is gone," said Gray, "and has left me in far worse company." Many a poet complains truculantly of the way the "curse of verse" has of coming and going. Some day, perhaps through science, we may have a better understanding of this translunar mystery. But one thing is certain now: it is useless to attempt to make real poems when the Muse has absented herself. As Keats wisely says, "If poetry comes not as naturally as the leaves of a tree, it had better not come at all."

Whether the theme of contemplation be God or human, nature or music or story, or a social passion of idealism, the poet must wait for his hour to come. Whether the shock of emotion which arouses the spirit of creation in him be pain or pleasure or mere conflict, he must bide his time.

And when his hour does come, he must use it to make
his masterpiece.   Then, if poetic genius be in him in
adequate measure, a spark will shine out of darkness,
flicker in pale flame, spread into glowing fire, and become
a warm peace to live forever in the mind of the race.

From "An Epistle to John Lapraik, an old Scottish Bard."

> But, first an' foremost, I should tell,
> Amaist as soon as I could spell,
> I to the crambo-jingle fell,
>   Tho' rude an' rough,
> Yet crooning to a body's sel',
>   Does weel eneugh.
>
> I am nae poet, in a sense,
> But just a rhymer, like, by chance,
> An' ha'e to learning nae pretence,
>   Yet, what the matter?
> Whene'er my muse does on me glance,
>   I jingle at her.
>
> Your critic-folk may cock their nose,
> And say, "How can you e'er propose,
> You wha ken hardly verse frae prose,
>   To mak a sang?"
> But, by your leaves, my learned foes,
>   Ye're maybe wrang.
>
> What's a' your jargon o' your schools,
> Your Latin names for horns an' stools;

If honest nature made you fools,
    What sairs your grammars?
Ye'd better ta'en up spades an' shools
    Or knappin' hammers.

A set o' dull, conceited hashes,
Confuse their brains in college classes!
They gang in stirks, and come out asses,
    Plain truth to speak;
An' syne they think to climb Parnassus
    By dint o' Greek!

Gi'e me ae spark o' Nature's fire,
That's a' the learning I desire;
Then though I drudge through dub and mire
    At pleugh or cart,
My muse, though hamely in attire,
    May touch the heart.

                              —*Robert Burns*

From "Works of Robert Burns." To Dr. Moore.

Indeed, I did not well know myself why I liked so much
to loiter behind with her, when returning in the evening
from our labours; why the tones of her voice made my
heart-strings thrill like an Æolian harp; and particularly
why my pulse beat such a furious rantann, when I looked
and fingered over her hand to pick out the nettle-stings
and thistles. Among her other love-inspiring qualifica-
tons, she sung sweetly; and 'twas her favourite Scotch
reel that I attempted to give an embodied vehicle to in

rhyme. I was not so presumptive as to imagine that I could make verses like printed ones, composed by men who had Greek and Latin; but my girl sung a song which was said to be composed by a small country laird's son, on one of his father's maids, with whom he was in love; and I saw no reason why I might not rhyme as well as he; for, excepting smearing sheep and casting peats (his father living in the moors), he had no more scholar-craft than I had. Thus with me began love and poesy; which at times have been my only, and till within this last twelve months, have been my highest enjoyment.

* * * * * *

My passions, when once they were lighted up, raged like so many devils till they got vent in rhyme; and then conning over my verses, like a spell, soothed all into quiet!

* * * * * *

The first of my poetic offspring that saw the light was a burlesque lamentation on a quarrel between two Reverend Calvinists, both of them *dramatis personæ* in my "Holy Fair." I had an idea myself that the piece had some merits; but, to prevent the worst, I gave a copy of it to a friend who was very fond of these things, and told him I could not guess who was the author of it, but that I thought it pretty clever. With a certain side of both clergy and laity, it met with a roar of applause. "Holy Willie's Prayer" next made its appearance, and alarmed the kirk-session so much that they held three several meetings to look over their holy artillery, if any of it was pointed against profane rhymers. Unluckily for me, my idle wanderings led me on another side, point-blank, within reach of their heaviest metal. This is the unfortunate story alluded to in my printed poem, "The Lament." 'Twas a shocking affair, which I cannot yet bear to recollect, and it had very nearly given me one or two of the principal qualifications for a place among those who have lost the chart, and mistaken the reckoning of rationality.

—*Robert Burns*

From "Works of Robert Burns." Motto Prefixed to the Author's First Publication.

The simple Bard, unbroke by rules of art,
He pours the wild effusions of the heart;
And if inspir'd, 'tis Nature's pow'rs inspire;
Her's all the melting thrill, and her's the kindling fire.

—*Robert Burns*

From "Works of Robert Burns." Robert Burns to George Thomson.

I find that I have still an hour to spare this morning before my conveyance goes away: I shall give you "Nannie, O," at length.

Your remarks on "Ewe-bughts, Marion," are just; still it has obtained a place among our more classic Scots songs; and what with many beauties in its composition, and more prejudices in its favor, you will not find it easy to supplant it.

In my very early years, when I was thinking of going to the West Indies, I took the following farewell of a dear girl. It is quite trifling, and has nothing of the merits of "Ewe-bughts"; but it will fill up this page. You must know that all my earlier love-songs were the breathings of ardent passion, and though it might have been easy in after times to have given them a polish, yet that polish to me whose they were, and who perhaps alone cared for them, would have defaced the legend of the heart, which was so faithfully inscribed on them. Their uncouth simplicity was, as they say of wines, their race.

—*Robert Burns*

From "Poems." Part of a preface.

. . . Of impassioned tenderness or Dionysiac frenzy I have nothing, nor even of that magic and pregnancy of phrase—really the creation of a fresh idiom—which marks the high lights of poetry. Even if my temperament had been naturally warmer, the fact that the English language (and I can write no other with assurance) was not my mother-tongue would of itself preclude any inspired use of it on my part; its roots do not quite reach to my centre. I never drank in in my childhood the homely cadences and ditties which in pure spontaneous poetry set the essential key. I know no words redolent of the wonder-world, the fairy-tale, or the cradle. Moreover, I am city-bred, and that companionship with nature, those rural notes, which for English poets are almost inseparable from poetic feeling, fail me altogether. Landscape to me is only a background for fable or a symbol for fate, as it was to the ancients; and the human scene itself is but a scheme for reflection. Nor have I been tempted into the by-ways even of towns, or fascinated by the aspect and humours of all sorts and conditions of men. My approach to language is literary, my images are only metaphors, and sometimes it seems to me that I resemble my countryman Don Quixote, when in his airy flights he was merely perched on a high horse and a wooden Pegasus; and I ask myself if I ever had anything to say in verse that might not have been said better in prose.

And yet, in reality, there was no such alternative. What I felt when I composed those verses could not have been rendered in any other form. Their sincerity is absolute, not only in respect to the thought which might be abstracted from them and expressed in prose, but also in respect to the aura of literary and religious associations which envelops them. If their prosody is worn and traditional, like a liturgy, it is because they represent the initiation of a mind into a world older and larger than itself; not the chance experiences of a stray individual, but his submission to what is not his chance experience; to the truth of nature and the moral heritage of mankind. Here is the uncertain hand of an apprentice, but of an apprentice in a great school. Verse is one of the traditions of literature. Like the orders of Greek architecture, the sonnet or the couplet or the quatrain are better than anything else that has been devised to serve the same function; and the innate freedom of poets to hazard new forms does not abolish the freedom of all men to adopt the old ones. It is almost inevitable that a man of letters, if his mind is cultivated and capable of moral concentration, should versify occasionally, or should have versified. He need not on that account pose as a poetic genius, and

yet his verses (like those of Michael Angelo, for instance)
may form a part, even if a subordinate part, of the expression of his mind. Poetry was made for man, not
man for poetry, and there are really as many kinds of it
as there are poets, or even verses. Is Hamlet's Soliloquy
poetry? Would it have conveyed its meaning better if
not reined in by the metre, and made to prance and turn
to the cadences of blank verse? Whether better or worse,
it would certainly not be itself without that movement.
Versification is like a pulsing accompaniment, somehow sus-
taining and exalting the clear logic of the words. The
accompaniment may be orchestral, but it is not necessarily
worse for being thrummed on a mandolin or a guitar.
So the couplets of Pope or Dryden need not be called
poetry, but they could not have been prose. They frame
in a picture, balanced like the dance. There is an elevation, too, in poetic diction, just because it is consecrated
and archaic; a pomp as of a religious procession, without
which certain intuitions would lose all their grace and
dignity. Borrowed plumes would not even seem an orna-
ment if they were not in themselves beautiful. To say
that what was good once is good no longer is to give
too much importance to chronology. Æsthetic fashions may
change, losing so much beauty at one end as they gain
at the other, but innate taste continues to recognise its
affinities, however remote, and need never change. Mask
and buskin are often requisite in order to transport what
is great in human experience out of its embosoming little-
ness. They are inseparable from finality, from perception of the ultimate. Perhaps it is this tragic finality that
English poets do not have and do not relish; they feel

it to be rhetorical. But verse after all is a form of rhetoric, as is all speech and even thought; a means of pouring experience into a mould which fluid experience cannot supply, and of transmuting emotion into ideas, by making it articulate.

In one sense I think that my verses, mental and thin as their texture may be, represent a true inspiration, a true docility. A Muse—not exactly an English Muse—actually visited me in my isolation; the same, or a ghost of the same, that visited Boethius or Alfred de Musset or Leopardi. It was literally impossible for me then not to reëcho her eloquence. When that compulsion ceased, I ceased to write verses. My emotion—for there was genuine emotion—faded into a sense that my lesson was learned and my troth plighted; there was no longer any occasion for this sort of breathlessness and unction.

—*George Santayana*

THE POET AND HIS MUSE

I sighed unto my Muse, "O gentle Muse,
   Would you but come and kiss my aching brow,
And thus a little life and joy infuse
   Into my brain and heart so weary now;
Into my heart so sad with emptiness
Even when unafflicted by the stress
     Of all our kinds poor life;
Into my brain so feeble and so listless
    Crushed down by burthens of dark thought resistless
     Of all our want and woe and unresulting strife.

"Would you but come and kiss me on the brow,
    Would you but kiss me on the pallid lips
That have so many years been songless now,
    And on the eyes involved in drear eclipse;
That thus the barren brain long overwrought
Might yield again some blossoms of glad thought,
        And the long-mute lips sing,
And the long arid eyes grow moist and tender
With some new vision of the ancient splendour
        Of beauty and delight that lives in everything.

"Would you but kiss me on the silent lips
    And teach them thus to sing some new sweet song;
Would you but kiss my eyes from their eclipse
    With some new tale of old-world right and wrong:
Some song of love and joy or tender grief
Whose sweetness is its own divine relief,
        Whose joy is golden bliss;
Some solemn and impassioned antique story
Where love against dark doom burns out in glory,
        Where life is freely staked to win one mutual kiss.

"Would you but sing to me some new dear song
    Of love in bliss or bale alike supreme;
Some story of our old-world right and wrong
    With noble passion burning through the theme:
What though the story be of darkest doom,
If loyal spirits shining through its gloom
        Throb to us from afar?

What though the song with heavy sorrows languish,
If loving hearts pulse to us through its anguish?
    Is not the whole black night enriched by one pure
        star?"

And lo! She came, the ever-gentle Muse,
    Sad as my heart, and languid as my brain;
Too gentle in her loving to refuse,
    Although her steps were weariness and pain;
Although her eyes were blank and lustreless,
Although her form was clothed with heaviness
    And drooped beneath the weight;
Although her lips were blanched from all their blooming,
Her pure face pallid as from long entombing,
    Her bright regard and smile sombre and desolate—

"Sad as thy heart and languid as thy brain
    I come unto thy sighing through the gloom,
I come with mortal weariness and pain,
    I come as one compelled to leave her tomb:
Behold, am I not wrapt as in the cloud
Of death's investiture and sombre shroud?
    Am I not wan as death?
Look at the withered leafage of my garland,
Is it not nightshade from the sad, dim, far land
    Of night and old oblivion and no mortal breath?

"I come unto thy sighing through the gloom,
    My hair dishevelled dank with dews of night,
Reluctantly constrained to leave my tomb;
    With eyes that have for ever lost their light;

My vesture mouldering with deep death's disgrace,
  My heart as chill and bloodless as my face,
    My forehead like a stone;
My spirit sightless as my eyes are sightless,
My inmost being nerveless, soulless, lightless,
    My joyous singing voice a harsh sepulchral moan.

"My hair dishevelled dank with dews of night,
  From that far region of dim death I come,
With eyes and soul and spirit void of light,
  With lips more sad in speech than stark and dumb:
Lo, you have ravaged me with dolorous thought
Until my brain was wholly overwrought,
    Barren of flowers and fruit;
Until my heart was bloodless for all passion,
Until my trembling lips could no more fashion
    Sweet words to fit sweet airs of trembling lyre and lute.

"From the sad regions of dim death I come;
  We tell no tales there for our tale is told,
We sing no songs there for our lips are dumb,
  Likewise our hearts and brains are graveyard mould;
No wreaths of laurel, myrtle, ivy or vine,
About our pale and pulseless brows entwine,
    And that sad frustrate realm
Nor amaranths nor asphodels can nourish,
But aconite and black red poppies flourish
    On such Lethean dews as fair life overwhelm.

"We tell no tales more, we whose tale is told;
  As your brain withered and your heart grew chill

My heart and brain were turned to churchyard mould,
  Wherefore my singing voice sank ever still:
And I, all heart and brain and voice, am dead;
It is my Phantom here beside your bed
    That speaketh to you now;
Though you exist still, a mere form inurning
The ashes of dead fires of thought and yearning,
    Dead faith, dead love, dead hope, in hollow breast
      and brow."

When It had moaned these words of hopeless doom,
  The Phantom of the Muse once young and fair,
Pallid and dim from its disastrous tomb,
  Of Her so sweet and young and *débonnaire,*
So rich of heart and brain and singing voice,
So quick to shed sweet tears and to rejoice
    And smile with ravishing grace;
My soul was stupified by its own reaping,
Then burst into a flood of passionate weeping,
    Tears bitter as black blood streaming adown my face.

"O Muse, so young and sweet and glad and fair,
  O Muse of hope and faith and joy and love,
O Muse so gracious and so *débonnaire,*
  Darling of earth beneath and heaven above;
If Thou art gone into oblivious death,
Why should I still prolong my painful breath?
    Why still exist, the urn
Holding of once-great fires the long-dead ashes,
No sole spark left of all their glow and flashes,
    Fires never to rekindle more and shine and burn?

"O Muse of hope and faith and joy and love,
  Soul of my soul, if Thou in truth art dead,
A mournful alien in our world above,
  A Phantom moaning by my midnight bed;
How can I be alive, a hollow form
With ashes of dead fires once bright and warm?
      What thing is worth my strife?
The Past a great regret, the Present sterile,
The Future hopeless, with the further peril
      Of withering down and down to utter death-in
        life.

"Soul of my soul, canst Thou indeed be dead?
  What mean for me if I accept their lore;
Thy words, O Phantom moaning by my bed,
  'I cannot sing again for evermore'?
I nevermore can think or feel or dream
Or hope or love—the fatal loss supreme!
      I am a soulless clod;
No germ of life within me that surpasses
The little germs of weeds and flowers and grasses
      Wherewith our liberal Mother decks the graveyard
        sod.

"I am half torpid yet I spurn this lore,
  I am long silent yet cannot avow
My singing voice is lost for evermore;
  For lo, this beating heart, this burning brow,
This spirit gasping in keen spasms of dread
And fierce revulsion that it is not dead,
      This agony of the sting:

What soulless clod could have these tears and sobbings,
These terrors that are hopes, these passionate throbbings?
    Dear Muse, revive! we yet may dream and love and
      sing!''

               —*James Thomson* (1834-1882)

From "A Ballad In Blank Verse."

Our ruthless creeds that bathe the earth in blood
Are moods by alchemy made dogmas of—
The petrification of a metaphor.
No creed for me! I am a man apart:
A mouthpiece for the creeds of all the world;
A soulless life that angels may possess
Or demons haunt, wherein the foulest things
May loll at ease beside the loveliest;
A martyr for all mundane moods to tear;
The slave of every passion; and the slave
Of heat and cold, of darkness and of light;
A trembling lyre for every wind to sound.
I am a man set by to overhear
The inner harmony, the very tune
Of Nature's heart; to be a thoroughfare
For all the pageantry of Time; to catch
The mutterings of the Spirit of the Hour
And make them known; and of the lowliest
To be the minister, and therefore reign
Prince of the powers of the air, lord of the world
And master of the sea. Within my heart
I'll gather all the universe, and sing
As sweetly as the spheres; and I shall be

The first of men to understand himself. . . .
And lo! to give me courage comes the dawn,
Crimsoning the smoky east; and still the sun
With fire-shod feet shall step from hill to hill
Downward before the night; winter shall ply
His ancient craft, soldering the years with ice;
And spring appear, caught in a leafless brake,
Breathless with wonder and the tears half-dried
Upon her rosy cheek; summer shall come
And waste his passion like a prodigal
Right royally; and autumn spend her gold
Free-handed as a harlot; men to know,
Women to love are waiting everywhere.

—*John Davidson*

From "Studies in Poetry," by Stopford A. Brooke (on Scott).

Deep pleasure in nature for her own sake was now universal in poetry. And when Scott had forgotten those elements in the modern world which he hated, and felt when as a child he read his first ballads; when he found himself in a place like the Trosachs, untrodden even by the foot of the shepherd, he flung himself into rejoicing, delightful, rich and keen description—frankly objective, never subjective, never weighted or involved with thought, always of the visible, never of the invisible beneath the visible, never of the spiritual underlying the material. Solitude made him happy, and, afar from men, his muse drew near to him, and then she smiled.

"My muse," he says, "will seldom wake,
Save by dim wood and silent lake;
She is the wild and rustic Maid,
Whose foot unsandall'd loves to tread
Where the soft greensward is inlaid
    With varied moss and thyme;

And, lest the simple lily-braid,
That coronets her temples, fade,
She hides her still in greenwood shade,
    To meditate her rhyme.
And now she comes! The murmur dear
Of the wild brook hath caught her ear,
    The glade hath won her eye;
She longs to join with each blithe rill
That dances down the Highland hill
    Her blither melody."

—*Sir Walter Scott*

From "Studies in Poetry," by Stopford A. Brooke (on Scott).

I am sure that the description of the revival of the
minstrel's spirit when he heard the long-forgotten melody
of his youth is the description of the temper of his own
soul.

But when he caught the measure wild
The old man raised his face, and smiled;
And lightened up his faded eye
With all a poet's ecstasy!
In varying cadence, soft or strong,
He swept the sounding chords along:
The present scene, the future lot,
His toils, his wants, were all forgot;
Cold diffidence, and age's frost,
In the full tide of song were lost;

Each blank, in faithless memory void,
The poet's glowing thought supplied:
And while his harp responsive rung,
'Twas thus the latest Minstrel sung.

—Sir Walter Scott

From "Pope's Works," Pope to Cromwell.

. . . I had I know not what extraordinary flux of rhyme upon me for three days together, in which time all the verses you see added have been written; which I tell you that you may more freely be severe upon them. It is a mercy I do not assault you with a number of original sonnets and epigrams, which our modern bards put forth in the spring-time in as great abundance as trees do blossoms, a very few whereof ever come to be fruit, and please no longer than just in their birth. So that they make no less haste to bring their flowers of wit to the press, than gardeners to bring their other flowers to the market, which, if they cannot get off their hands in the morning, are sure to die before night. Thus the same reason that furnishes Common (Covent) Garden with those nosegays you so delight in, supplies the muses' Mercury, and British Apollo, not to say Jacob's Miscellanies, with verses. And it is the happiness of this age that the modern invention of printing poems for pence a-piece has brought the nosegays of Parnassus to bear the same price; . . .

—Alexander Pope

From "Specimens of the Table Talk of Coleridge."

The best sort of music is what it should be—sacred; the next best, the military, has fallen to the lot of the Devil.

Good music never tires me, nor sends me to sleep. I feel physically refreshed and strengthened by it, as Milton says he did.

—*Samuel Taylor Coleridge*

From the preface to "Poems on Various Subjects."

Why then write Sonnets or Monodies? Because they give me pleasure when perhaps nothing else could. After the more violent emotions of Sorrow, the mind demands solace and can find it in employment alone; but full of its late sufferings, it can endure no employment not connected with those sufferings. Forcibly to turn away our attention to other subjects is a painful and in general an unavailing effort.

> "But O! how grateful to a wounded heart,
>   The tale of misery to impart;
> From others' eyes bid artless sorrows flow,
> And raise esteem upon the base of woe!"

—*Shaw*

The communicativeness of our nature leads us to describe our own sorrows; in the endeavor to describe them intellectual activity is exerted; and by a benevolent law of our nature from intellectual activity a pleasure results, which is gradually associated and mingles as a corrective with the painful subject of the description. "True!" it may be answered, "but how are the PUBLIC interested in your sorrows or your description?" We are for ever attributing a personal unity to imaginary aggregates. What is the PUBLIC but a term for a number of scattered individuals of whom as many will be interested in these sorrows as have experienced the same or similar?

> "Holy be the Lay
> Which mourning soothes the mourner on his way!"

There is one species of egotism which is truly disgusting; not that which leads us to communicate our feelings to others, but that which would reduce the feelings of others to an identity with our own. The Atheist, who exclaims "Pshaw!" when he glances his eye on the praises of Deity, is an Egotist: an old man, when he speaks contemptuously of love-verses, is an Egotist: and your sleek favourites of Fortune are Egotists, when they condemn all "melancholy, discontented" verses.

Surely it would be candid not merely to ask whether the Poem pleases ourselves, but to consider whether or no there may not be others to whom it is well-calculated to give an innocent pleasure. With what anxiety every fashionable author avoids the word *I*!—now he transforms himself into a third person—"the present writer"—now multiplies himself and swells into *"we"*—and all this is the watchfulness of guilt. Conscious that this said *I* is perpetually intruding on his mind and that it monopolizes his heart, he is prudishly solicitous that it may not escape from his lips.

—Samuel Taylor Coleridge

From "Letters of Samuel Taylor Coleridge." To Joseph Cottle.
The object of my present reply is to state the case just as it is. First, that for ten years the anguish of my spirit has been indescribable, the sense of my danger staring,

but the consciousness of my *Guilt* worse, far worse than all. I have prayed, with drops of agony on my brow, trembling not only before the justice of my Maker, but even before the mercy of my Redeemer. "I gave thee so many talents, what hast thou done with them?" Secondly, overwhelmed as I am with a sense of my direful infirmity, I have never attempted to disguise or conceal the cause. On the contrary, not only to friends have I stated the whole case with tears and the very bitterness of shame, but in two instances I have warned young men, mere acquaintances, who had spoken of having taken laudanum, of the direful consequences, by an awful exposition of the tremendous effects on myself.

—Samuel Taylor Coleridge

From "Disaster and Poetry." Concerning James Thomson (1834-1882).

For all except the bigoted moralist, at certain points life becomes a sort of madness. Browning with his sanity felt this, as *Porphyria's Lover* and *Johannes Agricola* testify. Toward the end Thomson had reached an age when there might not only arise some natural process of disease, but also the age when climax of some sort was inevitable. With some pathological personalities one can never tell when and to what extent the personality will break down. It depends on the depth of the invasion of disease. Often such men and women know nothing of the body. It is as if the science of the body or the human mechanism itself did not exist. The social and individual preciousness of that less than a cubic inch of cerebral cortex, bearing, as it does, its freight of memories individual and racial, human desires and human ideals, penitence, pity, hate and love, all that composes that incorporeal something we call human personality,—this is to them a fact unknown. While they defy many or all of the laws governing the body, they will discuss with intelligence the use of rays of light as a means towards interplanetary communication! Nature has many and unguessed-at intentions among her purposes. In man she would seem to intend something intellectual. This body blind-spot among men of genius may be one of Nature's means towards achieving an end at any cost. Who knows!

It is possible that a good deal of narcotized writing has seemed beautiful because its motivating power was not understood. Certain types of insanity have from time immemorial been stamped as divine inspiration, and so worshiped, for example, take epilepsy. Temporary mental disease is not creative inspiration. The creative instinct of the mind is as normal and as much a part of the expression of life as the physical creative instinct. It is true that conditions of health and disease mentally often merge into one another in a way that is bewildering. In the life of nature disease consumes even as in ours. Mentally, what does this mean in human experience? What is disease? Is it natural? That which takes away from the energy of the individual or the community is evil; that which adds to it is good. But in individual cases which does add more to the energy of the community, genius with some of its roots all too frequently embedded in disease, or perfect health without the genius? A dark problem and a bitter battleground! The taint of disease has for all except the pathologist and the psychoanalyst the lure of

the mysterious and is identified too frequently with greatness which in itself it is not, although it may be correlated
with greatness. Those who worship these gods in poetry
and prose without taking thought are no further advanced
in the social development of an art than the primitive tribe
worshiping awestruck before an epileptic chief can be
said to be advanced in religious experience.

In any event, the nearer disease and death press on a
sensitive mind perhaps all the more passionately does that
mind press towards the consolation of art which is immortal. It was for his singer's heart Thomson cared the
most. And it was his tragedy rather than anything more
personal or sentimental. Even as he was tortured he sang:
it is the old fable forever new, for James Thomson belonged
to the class of human beings who seem to rush from wreck
to wreck of their own making and who in the process of
destroying themselves gain a sort of inexplicable super-
power creatively.

—*Jeannette Marks*

From "Letters and Journals of Byron," by Moore.

It was, indeed, not without truth, said of him by Goëthe,
that he was inspired by the Genius of Pain—for, from the
first to the last of his agitated career, every fresh recruit-
ment of his faculties was imbibed from that bitter source.
His chief incentive, when a boy, to distinction was, as
we have seen, that mark of deformity on his person, by
an acute sense of which he was first stung into the ambition
of being great. As, with evident reference to his own fate,
he himself describes the feeling—

"Deformity is daring,
It is its essence to o'ertake mankind
By heart and soul, and make itself the equal,
Ay, the superior of the rest. There is
A spur in its halt movements, to become
All that the others cannot, in such things
As still are free to both, to compensate
For step-dame Nature's avarice at first."

—Lord Byron

From "Letters and Journals of Byron," by Moore. To Thomas
Moore.

. . . It is my intention to remain at Venice during
the winter, probably, as it has always been (next to the
East) the greenest island of my imagination. It has not
disappointed me; though its evident decay would, perhaps,
have that effect upon others. But I have been familiar
with ruins too long to dislike desolation. Besides, I have
fallen in love, which, next to falling into the canal (which
would be of no use, as I can swim) is the best or the worst
thing I could do.

* * * * *

By way of divertisement, I am studying daily, at an
Armenian monastery, the Armenian language. I found
that my mind wanted something craggy to break upon;
and this—as the most difficult thing I could discover here
for an amusement—I have chosen, to torture me into attention. It is a rich language, however, and would amply
repay any one the trouble of learning it. I try, and shall
go on; but I answer for nothing, least of all for my intentions or my success. . . .

—Lord Byron

From "Letters and Journals of Byron," by Moore.

The poet Cowper, it is well known, produced that master-piece of humour, John Gilpin, during one of his fits of morbid dejection, and he himself says, "Strange as it may seem, the most ludicrous lines I ever wrote have been writ-ten in the saddest mood, and but for that saddest mood, perhaps, had never been written at all.

From "Letters of George Meredith," to William Hardman.

MY DEAR LORD ABBOT:—I am working mightily. Last night I awoke, and at 3 o'clock struck a light and wrote a poem on Cleopatra for the "Cornhill," to suit Sandys's illustration. Also an "Ode" to the Napiers (part of it) and part of "The Ex-Champion's Lament." I say, young Copperfield! I never had such a fit on me since the age of 21; and my good love, waking too, joyfully assisted by lending notepaper and soothing me for having disturbed her slumber.

—George Meredith

TO SEANCHAN

In "At the King's Threshold," by William Butler Yeats.

> We have been too humble, Seanchan,
> Humble as you were proud;
> We have left the royal table
> For the platters of the crowd;
> And we eat what they have broken,

And we drink what they will leave,
But we hear when they have spoken
And we suffer when they grieve.

                                    —*Marguerite Wilkinson*

From "Tamburlaine the Great."
    If all the pens that ever poets held
    Had fed the feeling of their masters' thoughts,
    And every sweetness that inspired their hearts,
    Their minds, and muses on admirèd themes;
    If all the heavenly quintessence they still
    From their immortal flowers of poesy
    Wherein, as in a mirror, we perceive
    The highest reaches of a human wit:—
    If these had made one poem's period,
    And all combined in beauty's worthiness,
    Yet should there hover in their restless heads
    One thought, one grace, one wonder, at the least,
    Which into words no virtue can digest.

                                    —*Christopher Marlowe*

From "Timon of Athens."
    Painter.   You are rapt, sir, in some work, some dedica-
        tion
To the great lord.
    Poet.   A thing slipp'd idly from me.
Our poesy is as a gum, which oozes
From whence 'tis nourish'd; the fire i' the flint
Shows not till it be struck; our gentle flame

Provokes itself and like the current flies
Each bound it chafes.

—William Shakespeare

From "On English Poetry."

A poet reveals to a friend in a fit of excitement, "I say, listen, I am going to write a great poem on such-and-such! I have the whole thing clear in my mind, waiting to be put down." But if he goes on to give a detailed account of the scheme, then the act of expression (especially prose expression) kills the creative impulse by presenting it prematurely with too much definiteness. The poem is never written. It remains for a few hopeless days as a title, a couple of phrases and an elaborate scheme of work, and is then banished to the lumber room of the mind; later it probably becomes subsidiary to another apparently irrelevant idea and appears after a month or two in quite a different shape, the elaboration very much condensed, the phrase altered and the title lost.

Now this section is as suitable as any other for the prophecy that the study of Poetry will very soon pass from the hands of grammarians, prosodists, historical research men, and such-like, into those of the psychologists. And what a mess they'll make of it; to be sure!

—Robert Graves

Sculpture is particularly good for the mind: there is a height and divine stillness about it which preaches peace to our stormy passions. Methinks that, in looking upon a great statue like the Theseus (maim'd and defaced as it is), one becomes as it were Godlike, to feel things in the Idea.

Thro' darkness and storm and weariness of mind and of body is there built a passage for His created ones to the gates of light.

—*Alfred Tennyson*

A STATUE OF MINERVA

From "Prose Works."

The arm restored. The head is of the very highest beauty. It has a close helmet, from which the hair delicately parted on the forehead, half escapes. The face uplifted gives effect to the perfect form of the neck, and to that full and beautiful moulding of the lower part of the face and the jaw, which is, in living beings, the seat of the expression of a simplicity and integrity of nature. Her face uplifted to Heaven is animated with a profound, sweet and impassioned melancholy, with an earnest, fervid and disinterested pleading against some vast and inevitable wrong: it is the joy and the poetry of sorrow, making grief beautiful, and giving to that nameless feeling which from the imperfection of language we call pain, but which is not all pain, those feelings which make not only the possessor but the spectator of it prefer it to what is called pleasure, in which all is not pleasure. It is difficult to think that the head, though of the highest ideal beauty, is the head of Minerva, although the attributes and attitude of the lower part of the statue certainly suggest that idea. The Greeks rarely in their representations of the Divinities (unless we call the poetic enthusiasm of Apollo a mortal passion) expressed the disturbance of human feelings; and here is deep and impassioned grief, animating a divine countenance. It is indeed divine, as Wisdom which as Minerva it may be supposed to emblem, pleading earnestly with Power, and invested with the expression of that grief because it must ever plead so vainly. An owl is sitting at her feet. The drapery of the statue, the gentle beauty of the feet and the grace of the attitude are what may be seen in many other statues belonging to that astonishing era which produced it;—such a countenance is seen in few.

—Percy Bysshe Shelley

From "Letters of Percy Bysshe Shelley," by Ingpen. To Mary Wollstonecraft Shelley.

. . . I spent three hours this morning principally in the contemplation of the Niobe, and of a favorite Apollo; all worldly thoughts and cares seem to vanish from before the sublime emotions such spectacles create; and I am deeply impressed with the great difference of happiness enjoyed by those who live at a distance from these incarnations of all that the finest minds have conceived of beauty, and those who can resort to their company at pleasure. What should we think if we were forbidden to read the great writers who have left us their works? And yet to be forbidden to live at Florence or Rome is an evil of the same kind of scarcely less magnitude.

—Percy Bysshe Shelley

From "Letters of Percy Bysshe Shelley." To John Gisborne.

I write little now. It is impossible to compose except under the strong excitement of an assurance of finding sympathy in what you write. Imagine Demosthenes reciting a Philippic to the waves of the Atlantic. Lord Byron is in this respect fortunate. He touched a chord to which a million hearts responded, and the coarse music which he produced to please them, disciplined him to the perfection to which he now approaches. . . .

—*Percy Bysshe Shelley*

From "A Defense of Poetry."

Poetry turns all things to loveliness; it exalts the beauty of that which is most beautiful, and it adds beauty to that which is most deformed; it marries exultation and horror, grief and pleasure, eternity and change; it subdues to union, under its light yoke, all irreconcilable things. It transmutes all that it touches, and every form moving within the radiance of its presence is changed by wondrous sympathy to an incarnation of the spirit which it breathes: its secret alchemy turns to potable gold the poisonous waters which flow from death through life; it strips the veil of familiarity from the world, and lays bare the naked and sleeping beauty, which is the spirit of its forms.

—*Percy Bysshe Shelley*

THE ARGUMENT OF HIS BOOK

I sing of *Brooks, of Blossomes, Birds, and Bowers:*
Of *April, May,* of *June,* and *July*-Flowers.
I sing of *May-poles, Hock-carts, Wassails, Wakes,*
Of *Bride-grooms, Brides,* and of their *Bridall-cakes.*
I write of *Youth,* of *Love,* and have Accesse
By these, to sing of cleanly-*Wantonnesse.*
I sing of *Dewes,* of *Raines,* and piece by piece
Of *Balme,* of *Oyle,* of *Spice,* and *Amber-Greece.*
I sing of *Times trans-shifting;* and I write
How *Roses* first came *Red,* and *Lillies White.*
I write of *Groves,* of *Twilights,* and I sing
The Court of *Mab,* and of the *Fairie-King.*
I write of *Hell;* I sing (and ever shall)
Of *Heaven,* and hope to have it after all.

—*Robert Herrick*

THEMES FOR POEMS

How shall a poet choose his theme? Shall he study the encyclopædia as Agamemnon did in the "Peterkin Papers," all for the sake of an education? Shall he "write a poem about the beautiful sunset" at the suggestion of some woman like the one who "quacked" beside Rupert Brooke in the wood and was properly cursed for it? Shall he learn the fashion of the moment and then try to do better with it than other poets have done? Should he even listen to the King as Dryden once did? Not by any means! If he be a real poet, he will accept dry and stuffy learning only that he may assimilate it and then forget it,—as he would accept plain food. He will treat trite suggestions from prosaically effusive ladies with the rich red wrath that is appropriate to them. He will be so completely absorbed in his own intellectual and spiritual interests that changing fashions of thought and form will mean little to him as affecting himself. And as for Kings—he will be the one to make suggestions! He will know, as Padraic Colum knows, that

Intensity of feeling can only come from personal, from novel experience. Without personal, without novel experience, we may say that there will be no liveliness of movement in the poem.

He will agree with Emerson that

If your subject do not appear to you the flower of the world at this moment, you have not rightly chosen it.

And he will follow the advice given by Mr. Yeats:

> Beloved, gaze in thine own heart,
> The holy tree is growing there.

From that holy tree of life will drop down before his vision the bright fruit of his living thought, his magnetic feeling. Of that he will make his poems.

According to his temperament, and consciously or unconsciously, he is likely to take either one of two attitudes toward the choice of his themes. If he be temperamentally conservative, a lover of the great traditions of the past, a believer in law; if he must build up in his mind a thick wall between arts and fine arts, between the secular and the sacred; if he worships what is remotely and purely transcendent, then he is likely to think that certain themes are more appropriately used in poetry than others ever could be. He will like to write of stars and flowers and love and death, of Helen's eyes and Troy's towers, of arms and the man, of conventional religious experiences and attitudes. But if he be a libertarian, or even a liberal, giving room to the present and the future in his eternity; if he believes that arts become fine arts by becoming fine; if he thinks of all secular things as of sacraments, and therefore finds them sacred; if his God is intimately immanent, then, like Peter of old, he will call nothing common or unclean, and like Whitman he will be the poet of the body as of the soul. He will assert, perhaps he will even prove, that all themes are themes for poems when genius kindles to them. And it is the greater genius, I think, that claims the world and all things in it, for poetry, knowing that a rusty nail in a carpenter's pocket shares a planet's ordered flight through space and obeys the law that draws us nearer to the sun or holds us away from Betelguese.

An ever increasing number of modern poets belong to this second group. Elizabeth Barrett Browning, who has not yet lost her prestige among women of genius believed that we should have new forms as well as new thoughts in poetry and that if poets are not able to create them with power and glory and honor, then indeed poetry is grown weary and decrepit before its time. She was convinced that the poet should look always toward life and find his themes in all reality. She knew that poetry is everywhere —for the poet. Nor was this mental attitude due to any insecurity in culture of the kind that reactionaries complain of in our contemporary poets, for Mrs. Browning read her Greeks as few modernists can. Her opinion was the result of a ripe culture that understands the present and the future through the past and praises what is new because it has fathomed the old. In a similar way Emerson says that

The test or measure of poetic genius is the power to read the poetry of affairs,—to fuse the circumstance of to-day; not to use Scott's antique superstitions, or Shakespeare's.

He says:

This contemporary insight is transubstantiation, the conversion of daily bread into the holiest symbols.

And he regrets that the American life storming around him should be slow to find a tongue.

Whitman is even more emphatic, and more vivid, in his reiteration of the idea that the world belongs to the poet to be used in poems as he pleases. And he calls on the Muse to migrate from Greece and Ionia, from Jerusalem and Jaffa, so that entering in at our ports, probably at Ellis Island, she may sing the new songs of a new land, "amid the measureless grossness and the slag" and "a song no poet yet has chanted."

These are strong voices speaking strongly, and they have been influential. In our own period there has been a strong reaction, not imitative, I think, though it has been nearly unanimous, against many of the subjects definitely associated with poetry in the past. Many poets have tried to use the hitherto unassimilated experiences and the still imperfectly understood types of our modern civilization, or lack of civilization, as subjects for their poems. They have succeeded only sometimes, as would be expected, but that is an achievement. Much of what has been made out of new themes is bizarre and trivial, but much is vigorous, audacious, full of keen irony and brilliance. A few poems, because they have been written by poets with a personal capacity for greatness, have the proud values of dignity and insight. Only the poet of ample mind and heart can discover in unaccustomed places that poetry which is inherent in all things, and then, fresh from his discovery, make it known effectively. Only a Masefield, or a Moody, or a Robinson, can realize that men have died many deaths since Chaucer's day and have taken part in many resurrections. Only poets of this caliber can so realize minute and momentous changes made by time as to enable us to share life, and death, and resurrection. Only great poets can carry yesterday upon their shoulders while they climb uphill through to-day and point us toward to-morrow.

So it comes to pass that even now there are hints of another reaction. . . . As there was a reaction against mythology and nature when Moody wrote Gloucester Moors and Edwin Markham wrote "The Man with the Hoe," and Margaret Widdemer, Florence Wilkinson, Harriet Monroe, Eunice Tietjens and others made their several contributions to the poetry of industrial life; as there was another reaction against "cosmic" poetry, whatever that may be, when imagism began to flourish, and then again a reaction against sense impressionism in favor of realistic character study; so now there seems to be a slight reaction against all the themes called modern, and a desperate hunt for traditions that will meet modern needs. Many a young radical who would never think of reading the Bible for devotional purposes, or even for spiritual instruction, since we are too wise, nowadays, to seek spiritual instruction, nevertheless reads the Bible to find themes for poems! Scriptural personalities emerge somewhat damaged in contemporary poetry, but, after all, such reputations are safe enough to admit of nonchalance. Biblical characters are not treated discourteously because there is any grudge against them, but merely because the intense love of realism which dominates the intellectual life of the period has set aside—perhaps only for a day or an hour—the microscope through which it has been wont to squint at contemporary pygmies, and is gazing through a clumsy telescope that magnifies the faults of ancient giants.

Perhaps the human mind, whether in the individual or the race, tends to pass through phases. Perhaps the somewhat pale romanticism and derivative sentimentality of that part of our early literature which grieved Emerson and Whitman had to give way to the brutal but very nearly honest realism with which we have recently become familiar. Perhaps this, in turn, may grow up into a well-founded idealism, fresh and indigenous, of a quality that need not shame a Milton or a Blake. It may be that we move always away from our discovered weak illusions, through a realism that hungers and thirsts after truths as they are, toward a wisdom that would recast life in a new and stronger mould, a wisdom like that of Robert Frost.

Superficial thinkers often confuse sentimentality with idealism. They are "ages and worlds apart." Sentimentality is soft and easy and regressive and timid—very timid. It follows the movement of the mind of the masses, and follows ingratiatingly. It is soothing syrup for intellectual and spiritual babes. It is sultry and scented. The rebellion against it brings in a healthy gust of realism, a breeze of rough truth to play havoc with sickliness. Realism is for people who are intellectually and spiritually mature. But idealism has passed through realism and come out on the far side. Idealism is firm of fiber and looks forward; it is costly and exceedingly audacious. It takes the lead alone, defies all precedent, is hated, mocked, flouted, persecuted because it is of and for the great. Although we may fail to recognize it when it is near us in the flesh, or even in a flesh of words, it is the ultimate gift which we should ask our poets to give America.

Emerson says that it is easy to repaint "the mythology of the Greeks, or of the Catholic Church, the feudal castle." It is not easy. For once we must have the temerity to challenge Emerson. Perhaps he did not know how difficult it is to revitalize an old theme. Harriet Monroe, whose acute and varied experiences with poets should serve to guide her into all truth in such matters, rightly says that it requires a special and peculiar magic to handle old themes successfully. Again let us admit that the poet

makes the poem; it is not made by the subject. So long
as the artist labors according to the dictates of his own
genius he will enrich the world in proportion to his own
power. He may write of buttons and rouge, of cheese-
factories and tenements, if he wishes to, or of Helen's
eyes and Troy's walls; he may even write of stars and
flowers and conquer men's hearts and minds by his own
unique gift of beauty, if he will only be strongly sincere,
starkly and utterly himself. For every book is a book of
revelation.

LXXVI

Why is my verse so barren of new pride,
So far from variation or quick change?
Why with the time do I not glance aside
To new-found methods and to compounds strange?
Why write I still all one, ever the same,
And keep invention in a noted weed,
That every word doth almost tell my name,
Showing their birth and where they did proceed?
O, know, sweet love, I always wrtie of you,
And you and love are still my argument;
So all my best is dressing old words new,
Spending again what is already spent:
    For as the sun is daily new and old,
    So is my love still telling what is told.

—*William Shakespeare*

From "Specimens of the Table Talk of Coleridge."
I have already told you that in my opinion the destruction of Jerusalem is the only subject now left for an epic

poem of the highest kind. Yet, with all its great capabilities, it has this one grand defect—that, whereas a poem, to be epic, must have a personal interest,—in the destruction of Jerusalem no genius or skill could possibly preserve the interest for the hero from being merged in the interest for the event. The fact is, the event itself is too sublime and overwhelming.

—*Samuel Taylor Coleridge*

From a preface to "Poems."

If I could judge of others by myself, I should not hesitate to affirm, that the most interesting passages in our most interesting Poems are those in which the author develops his own feelings. The sweet voice of Cona never sounds so sweetly as when it speaks of itself; and I should almost suspect that man of an unkindly heart, who could read the opening of the third book of the *Paradise Lost* without peculiar emotion. By a law of our Nature, he, who labours under a strong feeling, is impelled to seek for sympathy; but a Poet's feelings are all strong. *Quicquid amet valde amat*. Akenside therefore speaks with philosophical accuracy when he classes Love and Poetry, as producing the same effects:

"Love and the wish of Poets when their tongue
    Would teach to others' bosoms what so charms
Their own."—*Pleasures of Imagination*.

I shall only add that each of my readers will, I hope, remember that these poems on various subjects, which he reads at one time and under the influence of one set of feelings, were written at different times and prompted by very different feelings; and therefore that the supposed inferiority of one poem to another may sometimes be owing to the temper of mind in which he happens to peruse it.

—Samuel Taylor Coleridge

From "Life, Letters and Literary Remains of John Keats," by Milnes, 1848, to brother and sister.

. . . There is an electric fire in human nature, tending to purify; so that, among these human creatures, there is continually some birth of new heroism; the pity is, that we must wonder at it, as we should at finding a pearl in rubbish. I have no doubt that thousands of people, never heard of, have had hearts completely disinterested. I can remember but two, Socrates and Jesus. Their histories evince it. What I heard Taylor observe with respect to Socrates is true of Jesus: that, though he transmitted no writing of his own to posterity, we have his mind, and his sayings, and his greatness, handed down to us by others. Even here, though I am pursuing the same instinctive course as the veriest animal you can think of—I am, however, young and writing at random, straining after particles of light in the midst of a great darkness, without knowing the bearing of any one assertion, of any one opinion —yet, in this may I not be free from sin? May there not be superior beings, amused with any graceful, though instinctive, attitude my mind may fall into, as I am entertained with the alertness of the stoat, or the anxiety of the deer? Though a quarrel in the street is a thing to be hated, the energies displayed in it are fine; the commonest man shows a grace in his quarrel. By a superior Being our reasonings may take the same tone; though erroneous, they may be fine. This is the very thing in which consists Poetry, and if so, it is not so fine a thing as Philosophy, for the same reason that an eagle is not so fine a thing as truth. Give me this credit, do you not think I strive to know myself?

—*John Keats*

From "Table Talk."

From him who rears a poem lank and long,
To him who strains his all into a song;
Perhaps some bonny Caledonian air
All birks and braes, though he was never there;
Or having whelp'd a prologue with great pains,
Feels himself spent and fumbles for his brains;
A prologue interdash'd with many a stroke—
An art contriv'd to advertise a joke,
So that the jest is clearly to be seen,
Not in the words—but in the gap between;
Manner is all in all, whate'er is writ,
The substitute for genius, sense and wit.
To dally much with subjects mean and low
Proves that the mind is weak, or makes it so.
Neglected talents rust into decay,
And every effort ends in pushpin play.
The man that means success should soar above
A soldier's feather, or a lady's glove;
Else, summoning the muse to such a theme,
The fruit of all her labor is whipp'd cream.

As if an eagle flew aloft, and then—
Stoop'd from its highest pitch to pounce a wren.
As if the poet, purposing to wed
Should carve himself a wife in gingerbread.

—William Cowper

From "Letter to John Wilson," 1800.

You begin . . . with this observation, that nothing is a
fit subject for poetry which does not please. But here follows a question, does not please whom? Some have little
knowledge of natural imagery of any kind, and, of course,
little relish for it; some are disgusted with the very mention of the words pastoral poetry, sheep or shepherds; some
cannot tolerate a poem with a ghost or any supernatural
agency in it; others would shrink from an animated description of the pleasures of love, as from a thing carnal
and libidinous; some cannot bear to see delicate and refined feelings ascribed to men in low conditions in society
. . . others are disgusted with the naked language of some
of the most interesting passions of men, because either it
is indelicate, or gross, or vulgar. . . . Then there are pro-
fessional and national prejudices for evermore. Some take
no interest in the description of a particular passion or
quality, as love of solitariness, we will say, genial activity
of fancy, love of nature, religion, and so forth, because
they have (little or) nothing of it in themselves; and so
on without end. I return then to (the) question, please
whom? or what? I answer, human nature as it has been
(and ever) will be. But, where are we to find the best
measure of this? I answer, (from with) in; by stripping

our own hearts naked, and by looking out of ourselves to (wards men) who lead the simplest lives, and most according to nature; men who have never known false refinements, wayward and artificial desires, false criticisms, effeminate habits of thinking and feeling, or who having known these things have outgrown them. This latter class is the most to be depended upon, but it is very small in number.

—*William Wordsmorth*

From "Preface to Lyrical Ballads," 1802.

The objects of the poet's thoughts are everywhere; though the eyes and senses of men are, it is true, his favourite guides, yet he will follow wheresoever he can find an atmosphere of sensation in which to move his wings. Poetry is the first and last of all knowledge—it is as immortal as the heart of man. If the labours of men of science should ever create any material revolution, direct or indirect, in our condition, and in the impressions which we habitually receive, the poet will sleep then no more than at present; he will be ready to follow the steps of the man of science, not only in those general indirect effects, but he will be at his side, carrying sensation into the midst of the objects of the science itself. The remotest discoveries of the chemist, the botanist, or mineralogist, will be as proper objects of the poet's art as any upon which it can be employed, if the time should ever come when these things shall be familiar to us, and the relations under which they are contemplated by the followers of these respective sciences shall be manifestly and palpably material to us as enjoying and suffering beings. If the time should ever come when what is now called science, thus familiarized to men, shall be ready to put on, as it were, a form of flesh and blood, the poet will lend his divine spirit to aid the transfiguration, and will welcome the Being thus produced, as a dear and genuine inmate of the household of man.

—*William Wordsmorth*

From "Preface to Poems," 1853-1854.

"The poet," it is said, and by an intelligent critic, "the poet who would really fix the public attention must leave the exhausted past, and draw his subjects from matters of present import, and *therefore* both of interest and novelty."

Now this view I believe to be completely false. It is worth examining, inasmuch as it is a fair sample of a class of critical dicta everywhere current at the present day, having a philosophical form and air, but no real basis in fact. . . .

What are the eternal objects of poetry among all nations and at all times? They are actions; human actions; possessing an inherent interest in themselves, and which are to be communicated in an interesting manner by the art of the poet. Vainly will the latter imagine that he has everything in his own power; that he can make an intrinsically inferior action equally delightful with a more excellent one by his treatment of it: he may indeed compel us to admire his skill but his work will possess, within itself, an incurable defect.

The poet, then, has in the first place to select an ex-

cellent action; and what actions are the most excellent?
Those, certainly, which most powerfully appeal to the
great primary human affections: to those elementary feelings which subsist permanently in the race, and which are
independent of time. These feelings are permanent and
the same; that which interests them is permanent and the
same also. The modernness or antiquity of an action, therefore, has nothing to do with its fitness for poetical representation; this depends upon its inherent qualities. To the
elementary part of our nature, to our passions that which
is great and passionate is eternally interesting; and interesting solely in proportion to its greatness and to its passion. A great human action of a thousand years ago is
more interesting to it than a smaller human action of today,
even though upon the representation of this last the most
consummate skill may have been expended, and though
it has the advantage of appealing by its modern language,
familiar manners, and contemporary allusions, to all our
transient feelings and interests. These, however, have no
right to demand of a poetical work that it shall satisfy
them; their claims are to be directed elsewhere. Poetical
works belong to the domain of our permanent passions: let
them interest these, and the voice of all subordinate claims
upon them is at once silenced.

—*Matthew Arnold*

From "Poems, 1853-1854, Preface to the Second Edition."

It has been said that I wish to limit the poet in his choice
of subjects to the period of Greek and Roman antiquity:
but it is not so: I only counsel him to choose for his subjects

great actions, without regarding to what time they belong.
Nor do I deny that the poetic faculty can and does manifest
itself in treating the most trifling action, the most hopeless
subject. But it is a pity that power should be compelled
to impart interest and force to his subject, instead of receiving them from it and thereby doubling his impressive-
ness. There is, it has been excellently said, an immortal
strength in the stories of great actions: the most gifted
poet, then, may well be glad to supplement with it that
mortal weakness, which, in presence of the vast spectacle
of life and the world, he must for ever feel to be his individual portion.

—*Matthew Arnold*

From "Preface to Poems," 1853-1854.

A poetical work . . . is not yet justified when it has
been shown to be an accurate, and therefore interesting,
representation; it has to be shown also that it is a representation from which men can derive enjoyment. In presence of the most tragic circumstances, represented in a
work of art, the feeling of enjoyment, as is well known,
may still subsist: the representation of the most utter
calamity, of the liveliest anguish, is not sufficient to destroy
it: the more tragic the situation, the deeper becomes the
enjoyment; and the situation is more tragic in proportion
as it becomes more terrible.

What then are the situations, from the representation
of which, though accurate, no poetical enjoyment can be
derived? They are those in which the suffering finds no
vent in action; in which a continuous state of mental

distress is prolonged, unrelieved by incident, hope, or re-
sistance; in which there is everything to be endured,
nothing to be done. In such situations there is inevitably
something morbid, in the description of them something
monotonous. When they occur in actual life, they are
painful, not tragic; the representation of them in poetry
is painful also.

—*Matthew Arnold*

From "News from Nowhere," 1871.

[I]n the nineteenth century . . . there was a theory
that art and imaginative literature ought to deal with contemporary life; but they never did so; for, if there was
any pretence of it, the author always took care . . . to
disguise, or exaggerate, or idealize, and in some way or
another make it strange; so that, for all the verisimilitude
there was, he might just as well have dealt with the time
of the Pharaohs.

—*William Morris*

From "Essays and Studies," 1872.

The question whether past or present afford the highest
matter for high poetry and offer the noblest reward to the
noble workman . . . is really less debatable on any rational
ground than the question of the end and aim of art. . . .
Art knows nothing of time; for her there is but one tense,
and all ages in her sight are alike present; there is nothing
old in her sight, and nothing new. . . . [S]he cannot be
vulgarized by the touch of the present or deadened by the

contact of the past. . . . No form is obsolete, no subject
out of date, if the right man be there to rehandle it.

—Algernon Charles Swinburne

From "A Parallel of Poetry and Painting," 1695.

[A]ll stories are not proper subjects for an epic poem
or a tragedy. . . . The subjects . . . ought to have nothing
of immoral, low, or filthy in them. . . . I must add, that
though Catullus, Ovid, and others, were of another opinion,—that the subject of poets, and even their thoughts
and expressions, might be loose, provided their lives were
chaste and holy, yet there are no such licences permitted
in that art, any more than in painting, to design and colour
obscene nudities. *Vita proba est* is no excuse.

—John Dryden

From "Letters," 1758. To the Rev. W. Mason.

I must not have my fancy raised to that agreeable pitch
of . . . wild magical enthusiasm, and then have you let me
drop into moral philosophy and cold good sense. . . . Now
I insist that sense is nothing in poetry but according to
the dress she wears, and the scene she appears in.

—Thomas Gray

From "Family Letters of Christina Rosetti." To Dante
Rossetti.

[This letter is imperfect—the first sheet of it has been
lost. It would appear that Dante Rossetti had conveyed
to his sister a suggestion, made by Mr. Stillman, that she
should write some more poems, partaking (in greater or

less degree) of "politics or philanthropy." Such would not have been Rossetti's own recommendation: as he was more than commonly opposed to the use of such matter as a subject for poetry. Perhaps I need scarcely translate Christina's Italian words, *"tanto meglio per me,"* "so much the better for me."]

. . . It is impossible to go on singing out-loud to one's one-stringed lyre. It is not in me, and therefore it will never come out of me, to turn to politics or philanthropy with Mrs. Browning: such many-sidedness I leave to a greater than I, and, having said my say, may well sit silent. "Give me the withered leaves I chose" may include the dog-eared leaves of one's first, last, and only book. If ever the fire rekindles availably, *tanto meglio per me*: at the worst, I suppose a few posthumous groans may be found amongst my remains. Here is a great discovery, "Women are not Men," and you must not expect me to possess a tithe of your capacities, though I humbly—or proudly—lay claim to family-likeness. All this is for you, not for Mr. Stillman, for whom, however, are all our cordial regards. . . .

—*Christina Rossetti*

From "Fifine at the Fair."

A poet never dreams:
We prose-folk always do: we miss the proper duct
For thoughts on things unseen, which stagnate and obstruct
The system, therefore; mind, sound in a body sane,
Keeps thoughts apart from facts, and to one flowing vein

Confines its sense of that which is not, but might be,
And leaves the rest alone. What ghosts do poets see?
What demons fear? what man or thing misapprehend?
Unchecked, the channel's flush, the fancy's free to spend
Its special self aright in manner, time and place.
Never believe that who create the busy race
O' the brain, bring poetry to birth, such act performed,
Feel trouble them, the same, such residue as warmed
My prosy blood, this morn,—intrusive fancies, meant
For outbreak and escape by quite another vent!
Whence follows that, asleep, my dreamings oft exceed
The bound. But you shall hear.

—*Robert Browning*

From "The Works of Robert Burns." To George Thomson.

MY DEAR SIR: I fear for my songs, however a few
may please; yet originality is a coy feature in composition,
and, in a multiplicity of efforts in the same style, disap-
pears altogether. For these three thousand years, we
poetic folks have been describing the Spring, for instance,
and as the Spring continues the same, there must soon
be a sameness in the imagery, etc., of these said rhyming
folks. To wander a little from my first design, which was
to give you a new song, just hot from the mint, give me
leave to squeeze in a clever anecdote of my *Spring* originality:

Some years ago, when I was young, and by no means
the saint I am now, I was looking over, in company with
a *belle-lettre* friend, a magazine "Ode to Spring," when
my friend fell foul of the recurrence of the same thoughts,

and offered me a bet that it was impossible to produce an ode to Spring on an original plan. I accepted it, and pledged myself to bring in the verdant fields, the budding flowers, the crystal streams, the melody of the groves, and a love story into the bargain, and yet be original. Here follows the piece, and wrote to music, too!

ODE TO SPRING

Tune—"The tither morn," etc.
"When mauken bucks," etc.

See page 17, Vol. III.

A great critic (Aikin) on songs says, that Love and Wine are the exclusive themes for song-writing. The following is on neither subject, and consequently is no song; but will be allowed, I think, to be two or three pretty good prose thoughts inverted into rhyme:

SONG

"For a' that and a' that."
"Is there for honest poverty
  That hings his head, and a' that;
The coward-slave we pass him by;
  We daur be poor for a' that!"

—*Robert Burns*

From the preface to "The Seasons."

To insist no further on this head, let poetry once more be restored to her ancient truth and purity; let her be inspired from heaven, and, in return, her incense ascend thither; let her exchange her low, venal, trifling subjects for such as are fair, useful, and magnificent; and let her execute these so as at once to please, instruct, surprise,

and astonish; and then, of necessity, the most inveterate
ignorance and prejudice shall be struck dumb, and poets
yet become the delight and wonder of mankind.

* * * * *

Nothing can have a better influence towards the revival
of poetry than the choosing of great and serious subjects,
such as at once amuse the fancy, enlighten the head, and
warm the heart. These give a weight and dignity to the
poem, nor is the pleasure—I should say rapture—both
the writer and the reader feel, unwarranted by reason,
or followed by repentant disgust. To be able to write
on a dry, barren theme is looked upon by some as the sign
of a happy, fruitful genius—fruitful indeed! like one of
the pendent gardens in Cheapside, watered every morning
by the hand of the alderman himself. And what are we
commonly entertained with on these occasions, save forced,
unaffecting fancies, little, glittering prettinesses, mixed
turns of wit and expression, which are as widely different
from native poetry as buffoonery is from the perfection
of human thinking? A genius fired with the charms of
truth and nature is tuned to a sublimer pitch, and scorns
to associate with such subjects. * * *

I know no subject more elevating, more amusing, more
ready to awake the poetical enthusiasm, the philosophical
reflection, and the moral sentiment than the works of
Nature. Where can we meet with such variety, such
beauty, such magnificence?—all that enlarges and trans-
ports the soul? What more inspiring than a calm, wide
survey of them? In every dress Nature is greatly charm-

ing: whether she puts on the crimson robes of the morning, the strong effulgence of noon, the sober suit of the evening, or the deep sables of blackness and tempest. How gay looks the Spring, how glorious the Summer, how pleasing the Autumn, and how venerable the Winter. But there is no thinking of these things without breaking out into poetry; which is, by the by, a plain and undeniable argument of their superior excellence.

For this reason the best, both ancient and modern, poets have been passionately fond of retirement and solitude. The wild, romantic country was their delight. And they seem never to have been more happy than when, lost in unfrequented fields, far from the little, busy world, they were at leisure to meditate, and sing the works of Nature.

—*James Thomson* (1700-1748)

From "Marginalia."

In the hands of the true artist the theme, or "work," is but a mass of clay, of which anything (within the compass of the mass and quality of the clay) may be fashioned at will, or according to the skill of the workman. The clay is, in fact, the slave of the artist. It belongs to him. His genius, to be sure, is manifested, very distinctively, in the choice of the clay. It should be neither fine nor coarse, abstractly, but just so fine or so coarse, just so plastic or so rigid, as may best serve the purposes of the thing to be wrought, of the idea to be made out, or, more exactly, of the impression to be conveyed.

—*Edgar Allan Poe*

From "The Poetic Principle."

Thus, although in a very cursory and imperfect manner, I have endeavored to convey to you my conception of the Poetic Principle. It has been my purpose to suggest that, while this principle itself is, strictly and simply, the human aspiration for supernal beauty, the manifestation of the principle is always found in *an elevating excitement of the soul,* quite independent of that passion which is the intoxication of the heart, or of that truth which is the satisfaction of the reason; for, in regard to passion, alas! its tendency is to degrade rather than to elevate the soul. Love, on the contrary,—Love, the true, the divine Eros, the Uranian as distinguished from the Dionaean Venus,— is unquestionably the purest and truest of all poetical themes. And in regard to Truth, if, to be sure, through the attainment of a truth we are led to perceive a harmony where none was apparent before, we experience at once the true poetical effect; but this effect is referable to the harmony alone, and not in the least degree to the truth which merely served to render the harmony manifest.

—Edgar Allan Poe

THE MYTH OF ARTHUR

O learned man who never learned to learn
Save to deduce, by timid steps and small,
From towering smoke that fire can never burn
And from tall tales that men were never tall.
Say, have you thought what manner of man it is
Of whom men say, "He could strike giants down"?

Or what strong memories over time's abyss
Bore up the pomp of Camelot and the crown.
And why one banner all the background fills,
Beyond the pageants of so many spears,
And by what witchery in the western hills
A throne stands empty for a thousand years.
Who hold, unheeding this immense impact,
Immortal story for a mortal sin;
Lest human fable touch historic fact,
Chase myths like moths, and fight them with a pin.
Take comfort; rest—there needs not this ado.
You shall not be a myth, I promise you.

—*G. K. Chesterton*

From "Inspiration."

Thoughts let us into realities.   Neither miracle nor magic nor any religious tradition, not the immortality of the private soul is incredible, after we have experienced an insight, a thought.

—*Ralph Waldo Emerson*

From "Starting from Paumanok."

I will make the poems of materials, for I think they are
        to be the most spiritual poems,
And I will make the poems of my body and of mortality,
For I think I shall then supply myself with the poems
        of my soul and of immortality.

—*Walt Whitman*

From "Song of Myself."

I am the poet of the Body and I am the poet of the Soul,
The pleasures of heaven are with me and the pains of hell
      are with me,
The first I graft and increase upon myself, the latter I
      translate into a new tongue.

I am the poet of the woman the same as the man,
And I say it is as great to be a woman as to be a man,
And I say there is nothing greater than the mother of men.
                  —*Walt Whitman*

From "Song of The Exposition."

Come Muse migrate from Greece and Ionia,
Cross out please those immensely overpaid accounts,
The matter of Troy and Achilles' wrath, and Aeneas',
      Odysseus' wanderings,
Placard "Removed" and "To Let" on the rocks of your
      snowy Parnassus,
Repeat at Jerusalem, place the notice high on Jaffa's gate
      and on Mount Moriah,
The same on the walls of your German, French, and
      Spanish castles, and Italian collections,
For know a better, fresher, busier sphere, a wide, untried
      domain awaits, demands you.
                  —*Walt Whitman*

From "Song of The Universal."
    Come said the Muse,
    Sing me a song no poet yet has chanted,

Sing me the universal.
In this broad earth of ours,
Amid the measureless grossness and the slag,
Enclosed and safe within its central heart,
Nestles the seed perfection.

—*Walt Whitman*

We have grown extremely tired of Pan and other such talked-of gods of Greece; of Babylon and Arcadia and other more or less fabulous places; of Guinevere and Helen of Troy and Cleopatra—all the long-celebrated fascinators. It requires a special and peculiar magic to touch any of these enshrined idols without disaster, and with most modern poets the effort to do so is merely a pathetic appeal from the poverty of their own imaginations to the wealth that has been accumulated by the poets and artists of the past. It is essentially an insincerity, because it uses other people's experience and imagining instead of the poet's own. And a stern and stripped sincerity is a first essential of good art.

—*Harriet Monroe*

Intensity of feeling can only come from personal, from novel experience. Without personal, without novel experience, we may say that there will be no liveliness of movement in the poem. We have to be sure, then, that we have some intensity of feeling about the matter that is in our mind to be projected as a poem. It is personal, that is to say, it is not something that has been reported to you, but something that belongs to yourself: also it means more to you than anything else of the ten thousand happenings of the day. Feeling like this about the matter you may start to make your poem.

—Padraic Colum

A man who makes really good literature is like a fellow who goes into the field to pull carrots. He keeps on pulling them patiently enough until he finds a carrot that suggests something else to him. It is not shaped like other carrots. He takes out his knife and notches it here and there, until the two pronged roots become legs and the carrot takes on something of the semblance of a man. The real genius takes hold of that bit of life which is suggestive to him and gives it form. But the man who is merely a realist, and not a genius, will leave the carrot just as he finds it. The man who is merely an idealist and not a genius, will try to carve a donkey where no donkey is suggested by the carrot he pulls.

—Robert Frost

The poet comes to behold and to express the hidden loveliness of the world, to point out the ideal that is ever seeking to push through the husk of things and to reveal the inner spiritual reality. So all of life is material for his seeing eye and his thinking heart, and he makes the wonderful familiar and makes the familiar wonderful. . . .

We who have a serious purpose in our poetry, must, as far as possible, beware of the bare-bones of moral preach-

ment. We must not be so intent on capturing the truth
as to forget the beauty that is the veil of truth. Indeed,
beauty is so essential to truth that we do not really possess
the truth unless we have the beauty. So we are forced
to keep seeking until we find some symbol that will express
the beauty that is the eternal vesture of truth. This is
not always an easy task, yet it is the stern task that is laid
upon the poet by the austere Muse.

The poet must avoid the threadbare, the commonplace,
and the scientifically exact. He seeks to rise on the wings
of words to that high level where the kindled imagination
can create forms of ideal loveliness and find space for un-
hindered flight.

—*Edwin Markham*

JEWELLED BINDINGS

I have purloined my title, as I am fond of doing, from
the literary imagination of another, to whom my thanks
are hereby offered. John Webster furnished me with Nets
to Catch the Wind; I took Black Armour from Lionel
Johnson; to the anonymous author of an announcement
of a sale at the Anderson Galleries I am indebted for this
present caption. The phrase, as it originally stood upon
the pages of a fairly prominent review, was Superb Jewelled Bindings, but I am forced to let the sumptuous quali-
fication go the way of all too many brave things, and thus
sink into oblivion. The bindings of which I propose to
write are hardly superb, they are elaborate, neat, enamelled, elegant, perhaps exquisite, but they lack the vast

suavity of the truly superb in art. They are the bindings, the spiritual bonds, the sharp and delicately turned shapes and forms which so decoratively constrict the essence of contemporary lyric verse.

Permit me to quote from the picturesque bit of prose whence my title was stolen. "Surrounding this is a large wreath of laurel, tied with a mauve ribbon, and studded with fifty-eight pearls set in gold. Disposed around the cover are two hundred and twenty-three garnets and four opals. The design of the back cover is equally brilliant and contains forty-eight garnets, eight opals, eight moonstones, twenty-eight turquoises, twelve blue chalcedonies, two hundred and fifty-four amethysts, and nine topazes. There are scores of similar bindings, elaborate in design and lavish in the use of precious stones."

Surrounding what, you may well ask? At the Anderson Galleries all this intricacy surrounds Some Poems by John Keats, but in the curious museum of our own time some, nay many, poems by eminent young lyricists appear, if not similarly tied with mauve ribbon, at least painstakingly inlaid with seven moonstones and twelve blue chalcedonies. The large laurel wreath, though it has not yet been permanently awarded, has been bespoke by several, and he is poor indeed who cannot afford a few garnets and amethysts or a mild freshwater pearl.

So I figure us to myself, dwindled to the jewelled brightness of the picture in a camera obscura, hunched over our filing and fitting, careful lapidaries, clever goldsmiths, excellent workmen, for the most part, but a thought too intent upon the binding. Of course there are obvious exceptions; your personal predilections will supply their names. If I hesitate to say that I am one of the chief offenders, it is only because a writer's claim to distinction, even in crime, annoys the intelligent reader. So bowing always in the direction of the obvious exceptions —let me refer to us as a group, enchanted by a Midastouch or a colder silver madness into workers in metal and glass, in substances hard and brittle, in crisp and sharp-edged forms. From this company I exclude all persons whose poetry the Dial will publish, whether their lines rhyme or no. I include only the lyric poets, more or less young, entirely modern, who are, among a hundred and something million Americans, leaving little verse unto that enormous clan.

When I say little, I mean literally diminutive; short lines, clear small stanzas, brilliant and compact. I don't mean inferior or contemptible or negligible. Neither do I mean great.

One of the most enchanting conceits of the eighteenth century was the enamelled snuff-box, which opened to reveal not brown tobacco dust but a bright and singing bird. And although some few of our modern boxes have nothing but powdery dryness under their neat painted lids, most of them are music-boxes, whose gilded birds repeat a fine variety of tunes, melodious, bitter, passionate, or intellectual, as the case may be. And for this sort of singing a small jewelled receptacle of two or three well-polished stanzas is no bad thing; it is comfortable and fitting. Did I suspect for a moment, as in my own case I have not dared to suspect, that my bird was a live one, I should let him out.

I should let him out into freeedom, but not necessarily

into free verse. I should try to remember that he was born in a snuff-box, and be prepared to build him another house, a stone dovecote or a wicker cage, according to his nature. I should let him perch in the groves of Academe if he liked, or upon a bramble bush of ballads. If he were a real bird he would know his own mind, and his own music.

But the question remains unanswered, in my opinion at least, as to whether we have shut up any eagles or nightingales in our snuff-boxes. And I believe we are good workmen, dexterous and clean in our handling of gold and silver and precious—or even semi-precious—stones. I believe we are careful and conscientious, but not so much so as our detractors declare. I think rather that we have found a manner which very justly encloses our matter, a letter which very nicely defines our spirit. As to the decoration the setting of words transparent or opaque in a pattern upon our jewelled bindings, I am by no means ready to discard it. It is a deliberate art, perhaps, but as such it is a discipline and a struggle not to be too impetuously scorned. If our spirit is greater than the thing that holds it, it will go free of its own accord; our work is notoriously brittle, and I have no fear that its forms will ever imprison an authentic genius. And, in the remote possibility that some of us are not geniuses, but only adroit and talented young people with a passion for writing verse, it may be an excellent thing after all that we have cultivated a small, clean technique. A number of minor poets are far better employed in being brittle and bright and metallic than in being soft and opulently luscious. It keeps the workshop tidier, and leaves a little elbow-room

in which the very great may move their hammers and
chisels in serenity.

                                                —Elinor Wylie

From "The New Republic."

IMAGINATION

In all I have related hitherto imagination was not
present but only vision. These are too often referred to
as identical, and in what I have written I have tried to
make clear the distinction. If beyond my window I see
amid the manifolded hills a river winding ablaze with
light, nobody speaks of what is seen as a thing imagined,
and if I look out of a window of the soul and see more mar-
vels of shining and shadow, neither is this an act of imagination, which is indeed a higher thing than vision, and a
much rarer thing, for in the act of imagination that which
is hidden in being, as the Son in the bosom of the Father,
is made manifest and a transfiguration takes place like that
we imagine in the Spirit when it willed, "Let there be
light." Imagination is not a vision of something which
already exists, and which in itself must be unchanged by
the act of seeing, but by imagination what exists in latency
or essence is out-realized and is given a form in thought,
and we can contemplate with full consciousness that which
hitherto had been unrevealed, or only intuitionally sur-
mised. In imagination there is a revelation of the self
to the self, and a definite change in being, as there is in a
vapour when a spark ignites it and it becomes an inflamma-
tion in the air. Here images appear in consciousness which
we may refer definitely to an internal creator, with power

to use or remould pre-existing forms, and endow them with
life, motion and voice. We infer this because dream and
vision sometimes assume a symbolic character and a significance which is personal to us. They tell us plainly,
"For you only we exist," and we cannot conceive of what
is seen as being a reflection of life in any sphere. In
exploring the ancestry of the symbolic vision we draw nigh
to that clouded majesty we divine in the depths of our
being, and which is heard normally in intuition and con-
science, but which now reveals character in its manifestation as the artist in his work.

—*A. E.* (*George Russell*)

THE HARP

I have a harp of many strings
　But two are enough for me:
One is for love and one for death;
　And what would the third one be?

Before I learn another note
　I may forget and go,
So while my hand is light and sure
　I play on the strings I know.

—*Aline Kilmer*

*A BOOK

He ate and drank the precious words,
His spirit grew robust,

He knew no more that he was poor,
Or that his frame was dust;

He danced along the dingy days,
And this bequest of wings
Was but a book! What liberty
A loosened spirit brings!

—*Emily Dickinson*

PETIT, THE POET

Seeds in a dry pod, tick, tick, tick,
Tick, tick, tick, like mites in a quarrel—
Faint iambics that the full breeze wakens—
But the pine tree makes a symphony thereof.
Triolets, villanelles, rondels, rondeaus,
Ballades by the score with the same old thought:
The snows and the roses of yesterday are vanished;
And what is love but a rose that fades?
Life all around me here in the village:
Tragedy, comedy, valor and truth,
Courage, constancy, heroism, failure—
All in the loom, and oh, what patterns!
Woodlands, meadows, streams and rivers—
Blind to all of it all my life long.
Triolets, villanelles, rondels, rondeaus,
Seeds in a dry pod, tick, tick, tick,
Tick tick tick, what little iambics,
While Homer and Whitman roared in the pines!

—*Edgar Lee Masters*

A CAUTION TO POETS

What poets feel not when they make,
  A pleasure, in creating,
The world, in its turn, will not take
Pleasure in contemplating.

—*Matthew Arnold*

HOW POETS WORK

In the exquisitely written introduction to his "Colors of Life" Max Eastman gives a competent discussion of two methods of making poetry, the subjective method of Walt Whitman and the objective method of Edgar Allan Poe. He seems to prefer the method of Poe and quotes at length from the famous essay on the philosophy of composition in which we are told how the pertinaciously popular raven was made to croak his sardonic "Nevermore." But he also quotes some of Whitman's best lines, perhaps to show that the other method produces its own values.

Mr. Eastman could hardly have chosen more extremely divergent examples of the two ways of creating. Whitman, whose chief concern was to get himself said, typifies for our time the thought of poetry as a catharsis of the spirit. Poe, who was, by his own confession, an artist deliberate in every detail, considering always the impression to be made on a reader's mind, is a strong type of the craftsman at play with materials. Not many poets of rank are so confidently subjective as Whitman, so scrupulously objective as Poe.

Yet even Whitman was not merely subjective, even Poe was not entirely objective. Whitman must have rolled his resonant phrases through his mind and mouth for sheer joy in their amplitude. And Poe escapes the implications of the subjective only by dismissing them from consideration. He says:

Let us dismiss as irrelevant to the poem, *per se,* the circumstance—or say the necessity—which, in the first place, gave rise to the intention of composing a poem that should suit at once the popular and the critical taste.

Truly a believer in the subjective method might argue cogently that by the peremptory dismissal of circumstance and necessity Poe sets aside the underlying cause of all his choices, preferring to rationalize his thoughts and feelings, wishing to hide their origins even from himself. Modern psychology might make interesting suggestions with regard to both methods.

For it seems fairly obvious that the subjective poet is merely one who allows the subconscious mind free range in composition. Out of the deep he calls to his unknown gods and the volume and significance of his calling are often a surprise even to himself. The value of his work depends largely on the kind of a subconscious mind he has and on what he has put into it. Are the hidden springs sweet and clean, for the most part? If so, the fountains will rise white and glorious even though they be more unruly than those at Ashokan Dam. Are the hidden springs foul? The rising stream of thought will be darkened like a gush of crude oil near a coal mine. Whether the uprush be lovely or unlovely the poet of subjective method is seldom able to decide. He is rarely a good critic of his own work, for the elemental pleasure which he derives from the release of his own complexes often blinds him to defects in his way of saying things. If he were capable of the detachment essential to sound self-criticism, he would be too self-conscious about his own naive effusions to offer them whole-heartedly to the world in language. It is easy to believe that Whitman had no sense of humor, for we cannot laugh at our own incongruities until we know what is congruous. The peculiar danger of the poet who works subjectively, then, is variability, the alternation between the production of very good work sometimes, and of very bad work at other times.

The poet of objective method, on the other hand, tends to overwork the conscious intellect. He is critical and selective. He is never used by his inspiration, but uses it with taste and sensibility as a means to an end. (Sometimes he is so preoccupied with the making of phrases that he forgets it altogether.) He cunningly devises images of the objects of his worship, knowing perfectly well what they are and what they mean, hoping that mankind will bow down, not in ignorance as to idols, but with a recognition of the reality behind the symbol. The poet who works in this way is in danger of becoming artificial. "The Raven" is, to be sure, an interesting poem, perhaps the more interesting for being, in a large degree, the result of skill, but it is the less beautiful because it lacks other qualities which a somewhat less intellectual method might have given it. In the brief moods when it is still a bearable poem to me I am convinced that it was not composed altogether as Poe would have us believe, that something more warmly human than conscious cerebration entered into the making of it. But in general, and with due allowance for the fact that Poe's tongue may have been in his cheek when he wrote his "Philosophy of Composition," I accept most of what he tells us about its genesis,—and find it unbearable. Forever and forever the *tour de force* is likely to be brilliant rather than great.

Here we have the horns of the dilemma, the aesthetic dichotomy. But most of the masters seem to have chosen a middle way. Blake, who believed in inspiration and in the importance of the individual personality most emphatically was nevertheless a tireless craftsman. Although he claimed that "Improvement makes straight roads, but the crooked roads without improvement are roads of genius," he revised his poems after they were written and was far from scorning the difficult tricks of the poet's trade. William Butler Yeats who reaches out into the unseen, invokes the "elemental beings," and attempts to explore the racial memory with a mind avid of inspiration, spends hours in labor on his verse. Examples might be multiplied. The truth is that the poet whose chief desire is to offer us the vintage of a life should consider also the comeliness of the chalice, and the poet whose first thought is for the delicately jubilant task of making the cup should be sure that he can fill it with fine wine. Most great poets appear to use all the powers of personality, the body, the mind, and the spirit, in creation, fusing emotion, reason, and intuition, and thus producing beauty. They have broken down the barrier between the conscious and unconscious minds so that the fountain, when it rises, has all of its original energy and also takes the best direction. Sara Teasdale almost describes the process in the following words:

In the process of moulding his idea the poet will be at white heat of intellectual and emotional activity, bearing in mind that every word, every syllable, must be an unobtrusive and yet an indispensable part of his creation. Every beat of his rhythm, the color of each word, the ring of each rhyme, must conform inevitably to his feeling. By shaping his poem with perfect exactitude to hold his emotion, he fulfills his subsconcious aim in its composition.

If we ask ourselves how this transcendent diligence, this luminous efficiency can be achieved, we must find the answer in a great mass of varying experience, for no two poets seem to achieve it in exactly the same way. Some of them, like Robert Frost, write rapidly and make few alterations, but they make many, many poems which they regard as mere practise-work and throw away. William Butler Yeats not only works slowly and laboriously, but also makes many revisions even after publication. Poets of this type spare us much that we must suffer at the hands of the members of the "just-came-to-me" school of poetry who bury us under the avalanches of their loosened souls.

Yet it is well to remember with Coleridge that "poetry, like schoolboys, by too frequent and severe correction may be cowed into dullness!" Not every revision is an improvement. There is something to be said for the attitude of A. E., who writes of his own lyrics:

However imperfect they seemed, I did not feel that I could in after hours melt and remould and make perfect the form if I was unable to do so in the intensity of conception, when I was in those heavens we breathe for a moment and then find they are not for our clay.

Ben Jonson says that Shakespeare "never blotted a line," but that he himself in all friendliness wishes that he had blotted many, and gives good reasons for the wish. Yet we are content with Shakespeare because, in one way or another, he had made himself so Titanic a master of the mechanism of the creative mind that few of his lines needed to be blotted. For those that might better have been omitted he provided enormous compensation in others that the world will never give up.

Padraic Colum sums up the matter of the value of revision when he says:

Do not let your little poem run about too soon or it may become bandy-legged. Nurse it in your mind for many days and give it the blessing of the sun and moon and air and of the silence of night.

Only by waiting and wondering and making experiments can the poet learn what method of improving his work best serves his needs. And nobody else can teach him this, or learn it for him, for nobody else can know the subtle chemistry and physics of his mind and heart. The only axiom is: any way is a good way that makes a good poem. The only anathema is for the careless artist. A sincere artist cannot be slovenly in mind and heart and habit, although, because of defects in his powers of self-criticism, he may sometimes seem to be. Not all poets are capable of the detachment essential to astute criticism of their own work. Also, all poets are variable in creative ability as they are in their moods, and although it may be possible in June to make fifty sound and singing lines in a day, in July it may take three days to write three lines well. Yet the fifty lines may require no more real labor, and no less, than the three, since both represent not merely the time taken for setting them down on paper, but all the time spent beforehand in thought, study, feeling, and living, the time of preparation that really made them what they are.

That the act of utterance is the evidence of foregone study and experience should be obvious to everybody. If

there be no plums in Jack Horner's pie, he cannot pull
them out. Sidney says,

> Yet confess I always that as the fertilest ground must
> be manured, so must the highest flying wit have a
> Daedalus to guide him. That Daedalus . . . hath three
> wings to bear itself up into the air of due commendation:
> that is art, imitation and exercise.

This kind Daedalus can never be known save by those
whose minds are well stocked with the lore of the ages,
whether they get it from people or from books.

A poet may sometimes test the value of his work by ask-
ing himself how long the lines linger in his memory. The
lifeless verse moves toward death even in the mind of its
creator; the lively lines grow in memory. The more of a
craftsman a poet is, the more love he has bestowed on the
linking of words together, the more mnemonic value they
will be likely to have for him. Tennyson's son, writing a
memoir of his father, says:

> My Uncle Frederick writes: I am sure I could not per-
> form such a feat as I know Alfred to have done, any more
> than raise the dead. The earliest manuscript of the
> *Poems, Chiefly Lyrical*, he lost out of his great-coat
> pocket one night while returning from a neighboring
> market town. This was enough to reduce an ordinary
> man to despair, but the invisible ink was made to reappear,
> all the thoughts and fancies in their orderly series and
> with their entire drapery of words arose and lived again.
> I wonder what under such circumstances would become of
> the "mob of gentlemen who write with ease." Of course
> it would not much matter as they could easily indite some-
> thing new.
> My father's poems were generally based on some single
> phrase like "Someone had blundered": and were rolled

about, so to speak, in his head, before he wrote them down; and hence they did not easily slip from memory.

The making of poems is a work of intense and fiery quietness. Tennyson said, "I require quiet, and myself to myself more than any man when I write," but probably any good poet would say as much. That may be why the labor of making poems is often associated with the hours of the night when prolonged and uninterrupted meditation is possible. Amy Lowell is not the only midnight laborer. Consider Meredith's feat of writing three poems in one night; consider Whitwell Ellwin's narrative about Pope:

It was punctually required that his writing-box should be set upon his bed before he rose; and Lord Oxford's domestic related that, in the dreadful winter of Forty, she was called from her bed by him four times in one night to supply him with paper lest he lose a thought.

The night seems to be the orthodox time for making poems. Heterodox poets love the late afternoon hours when feverish activities of the day are in abeyance and when the slight fatigue of labor has produced a condition somewhat like that which comes after a moderate fast—a condition of receptiveness to incoming inspiration, or spiritual energy for expression. Each poet, according to the circumstances of his life and the mood and temper of his personality, has his own favorable times and seasons. When the creative mood comes upon him he must forget food and drink and life's lesser duties and pleasures, he must let the world slip into limbo that he may serve the Muse.

From "Colors of Life."

I think the essence of what we call classical in an artist's attitude is his quite frank acknowledgement that—whatever great things may come of it—he is at play. The art of the Athenians was objective and overt about being what it is, because the Athenians were educated, as all free men should be, for play.

*   *   *   *   *   *

And when we have arrived at a mood that is really and childly natural—a mood that will play, even with aspiration, and will spontaneously make out of interesting materials "things" to play with, and when in that mood we give our interest to the materials of reality in our own time, then perhaps we shall find that we have arrived also at a poetry that belongs to the people. For people are, in the depths of them and on the average as they are born, still natural, still savage. And there is no doubt that nature never fashioned them to work harder, or be more serious, or filled with self-conscious purports, than was necessary. She meant them to live and flow out upon the world with the bright colors of their interest. And it will seem rather a fever in the light of universal history, this hot subjective meaningfulness of everything we modern occidentals value. The poets and the poet-painters of ancient China knew that all life and nature was so sacred with the miracle of being that only the lucid line and color was needed to command an immortal reverence. They loved perfection devoutly, as it will rarely be loved, but they too, with their gift of delicate freedom in kinship with nature, were at play. And in Japan even today—

surviving from that time—there is a form of poetry that is objective and childlike, a making of toys, or of exquisite metrical gems of imaginative realization, and this is the only poetry in the world that is truly popular, and is loved and cultivated by a whole nation.

—*Max Eastman*

From "The Philosophy of Composition."

I prefer commencing with the consideration of an *effect*. Keeping originality *always* in view,—for he is false to himself who ventures to dispense with so obvious and so easily attainable a source of interest,—I say to myself in the first place, "Of the innumerable effects, or impressions, of which the heart, the intellect, or (more generally) the soul is susceptible, what one shall I, on the present occasion, select?" Having chosen a novel, first, and secondly a vivid effect, I consider whether it can be best wrought by incident or tone,—whether by ordinary incidents and peculiar tone, or the converse, or by peculiarity both of incident and tone,—afterward looking about me (or rather within) for such combinations of event, or tone, as shall best aid me in the construction of the effect.

I have often thought how interesting a magazine paper might be written by any author who would—that is to say, who could—detail, step by step, the processes by which any one of his compositions attained its ultimate point of completion. Why such a paper has never been given to the world, I am much at a loss to say; but, perhaps, the authorial vanity has had more to do with the omission than any one other cause. Most writers—poets in especial—

prefer having it understood that they compose by a species of fine frenzy—an ecstatic intuition—and would positively shudder at letting the public take a peep behind the scenes, at the elaborate and vacillating crudities of thought —at the true purposes seized only at the last moment—at the innumerable glimpses of idea that arrived not at the maturity of full view—at the fully matured fancies discarded in despair as unmanageable—at the cautious selections and rejections—at the painful erasures and interpolations—in a word, at the wheels and pinions—the tackle for scene-shifting—the step-ladders and demon-traps—the cock's feathers, the red paint and the black patches, which, in ninety-nine cases out of the hundred, constitute the properties of the literary *histrio*.

I am aware, on the other hand, that the case is by no means common, in which an author is at all in condition to retrace the steps by which his conclusions have been attained. In general, suggestions, having arisen pell-mell, are pursued and forgotten in a similar manner.

For my own part, I have neither sympathy with the repugnance alluded to, nor at any time the least difficulty in recalling to mind the progressive steps of any of my compositions; and, since the interest of an analysis, or reconstruction, such as I have considered a *desideratum*, is quite independent of any real or fancied interest in the thing analyzed, it will not be regarded as a breach of decorum on my part to show the *modus operandi* by which some one of my own works were put together. I select "The Raven" as most generally known. It is my desire to render it manifest that no one point in its composition is referable either to accident or intuition,—that the work proceeded, step by step, to its completion, with the precision and rigid consequence of a mathematical problem.

Let us dismiss, as irrelevant to the poem, *per se,* the circumstance—or say the necessity—which, in the first place, gave rise to the intention of composing *a* poem that should suit at once the popular and the critical taste. We commence, then, with this intention.

The initial consideration was that of extent. . . .

My next thought concerned the choice of an impression, or effect, to be conveyed: . . .

Regarding, then, Beauty as my province, my next question referred to the *tone* of its highest manifestation. . . .

The length, the province, and the tone, being thus determined, I betook myself to ordinary induction, with the view of obtaining some artistic piquancy which might serve me as a keynote in the construction of the poem,— . . .

—*Edgar Allan Poe*

From "Discoveries."

I remember, the Players have often mentioned it as an honour to *Shakespeare,* that in his writing, (whatsoever he penn'd) hee never blotted out line. My answer hath beene, would he had blotted a thousand. Which they thought a malevolent speech. I have not told posterity this, but for their ignorance, who choose that circumstance to commend their friend by, wherein he most faulted. And to justifie mine owne candour, (for I lov'd the man, and doe honour his memory (on this side Idolatry) as much as any). Hee was (indeed) honest, and of an open, and free nature: had an excellent *Phantsie* : brave notions, and

gentle expressions: wherein hee flow'd with that facility,
that sometime it was necessary he should be stop'd:
Sufflaminandus erat; as *Augustus* said of *Haterius.* His
wit was in his owne power, would the rule of it had beene
so too. Many times hee fell into those things, could not
escape laughter: As when hee said in the person of
Caesar, one speaking to him; *Caesar thou dost me wrong.*
Hee replyed: *Caesar did never wrong, but with just cause:*
and such like, which were ridiculous. But hee redeemed
his vices, with his vertues. There was ever more in him
to be praysed, then to be pardoned.

—Ben Jonson

From "Discoveries."

For a man to write well, there are required three Neces-
saries. To read the best Authors, observe the best Speak-
ers: and much exercise of his owne style. In style to consider what ought to be written; and after what manner;
Hee must first thinke, and excogitate his matter; then
choose his words, and examine the weight of either. Then
take care in placing, and ranking both matter, and words,
that the composition be comely; and to doe this with diligence and often. No matter how slow the style be at first,
so it be labour'd, and accurate; seeke the best, and be not
glad of the forward conceipts, or first words, that offer
themselves to us, but judge of what wee invent; and order
what wee approve. Repeat often, what wee have formerly
written; which beside, that it helpes the consequence, and
makes the juncture better, it quickens the heate of imagination, that often cooles in the time of setting downe, and

gives it new strength, as if it grew lustier, by the going
back. As wee see in the contention of leaping, they jumpe
farthest, that fetch their race largest: or, as in throwing
a Dart, or Iavelin, wee force back our armes, to make our
loose the stronger. Yet, if we have a faire gale of wind,
I forbid not the steering out of our sayle, so the favour
of the gale deceive us not. For all that wee invent doth
please us in the conception, or birth; else we would never
set it downe. But the safest is to returne to our Judge-
ment, and handle over againe those things, the easinesse of
which might make them justly suspected. So did the best
Writers in their Beginnings; they impos'd upon themselves
care and industry. They did nothing rashly. They obtain'd first to write well, and then custome made it easie,
and a habit. By little and little, their matter shew'd it
selfe to 'hem more plentifully; their words answer'd, their
composition followed; and all, as in a well-order'd family,
presented it selfe in the place. So that the summe of all
is: Ready writing makes not good writing; but good writing brings on ready writing: Yet when wee thinke wee
have got the faculty, it is even then good to resist it: as
to give a Horse a check sometimes with bit, which doth
not so much stop his course, as stirre his mettle. Againe,
whether a man's *Genius* is best able to reach thither, it
should more and more contend, lift and dilate it selfe, as
men of low stature, raise themselves on their toes; and so
oft times get even, if not eminent. Besides, as it is fit for
grown and able Writers to stand of themselves, and worke
with their owne strength, to trust and endeavour by their
owne faculties; so it is fit for the beginner and learner, to
study others, and the best. For the mind, and memory are

more sharpely exercis'd in comprehending an other man's things, then our owne; and such as accustome themselves, and are familiar with the best Authors, shall ever and anon find somewhat of them in themselves, and in the expression of their minds, even when they feele it not, be able to utter something like theirs, which hath an Authority above their owne.

—*Ben Jonson*

From "Discoveries."

There cannot be one colour of the mind; an other of the wit. If the mind be staid, grave, and compos'd; the wit is so, that vitiated, the other is blowne, and deflower'd. Doe wee not see, if the mind languish, the members are dull? Looke upon an effeminate person; his very gate confesseth him. If a man be fiery, his motion is so: if angry, 'tis troubled, and violent. So that wee may conclude: Wheresoever, manners, and fashions are corrupted; Language is. It imitates the publicke riot. The excesse of Feasts, and apparell, are the notes of a sick State; and the wantonnesse of language, of a sick mind.

—*Ben Jonson*

From the "Defense of Poesie."

Poesy . . . must be gently led, or rather it must lead. Which was partly the cause that made the ancient-learned affirm it was a divine gift, and no human skill: sith all other knowledges lie ready for any that hath strength of wit: a poet no industry can make, if his own *genius* be not carried unto it: and therefore is it an old proverb, *orator fit, poeta nascitur.* Yet confess I always that as the fertilest ground must be manured, so must the highest flying wit have a *Daedalus* to guide him. That *Daedalus*, they say, both in this and in other, hath three wings to bear itself up into the air of due commendation: that is, art, imitation, and exercise. But these, neither artificial rules nor imitative patterns, we much cumber ourselves withal.

—*Sir Phillip Sidney*

Seeds of Poetry and Rhime
　　Nature in my soul implanted:
But the genial Hand of Time
　　Still to ripen 'em is wanted;
Or, soon as they begin to blow
My cold soil nips the Buds with Snow.

If a plenteous Crop arise,
　　Copious numbers, swelling grain;
Judgment from the Harvest flies
　　And careless spares to weed the Plain:
Tares of Similes choak the roots,
Or Poppy-thoughts blast all the shoots.

Youth, his torrid Beams that plays,
　　Bids the poetick Spirit flourish;
But, tho' Flowers his ardour raise,
　　Maggots too 'twill form and nourish;
And variegated Fancy's seen
Vainly enamelling the Green.

First when Pastorals I read,
  Purling streams and cooling breezes
I only wrote of; and my head
  Rhimed on, reclined beneath the Tree-zes;
In pretty Dialogue I told
Of Phoebus' heat and Daphne's cold.

Battles, Sieges, Men and Arms,
  (If heroic Verse I'm reading)
I burn to write; with Myra's charms
  In Episode, to show my breeding:
But if my Myra cruel be
I tell her so in Elegy.

Tragick Numbers, buskin'd Strains,
  If Melpomene inspire,
I sing; but fickle throw my trains
  And half an act into the Fire;
Perhaps Thalia prompts a Sonnet
On Cloe's Fan, or Caelia's Bonnet.

For one Silk-worm thought that thrives
  Twenty more in Embrio dye;
Some spin away their little lives
  In ductile Lines of Foolery:
Then for a Moiety of the Year
Pent in a Chrysalis appear.

Till again the rolling Sun
  Bursts the inactive Shell, and thoughts

Like Butterflies, their Prison shun
　　Buzzing with all their parent Faults;
And, springing from the sluggish mould,
Expand their wings of flimzey Gold.

But, my Dear, these Flies, they say,
　　Can boast of one good quality;
To Phoebus gratefully they pay
　　Their little Songs and Melody;
So I to you this Trifle give,
Whose influence first bid it live.

　　　　　　　　　　　—Thomas Gray (?)

From "The Works of Robert Burns." To George Thomson.

"Laddie, lie near me," must *lie by me* for some time. I
do not know the air; and until I am complete master of a
tune, in my own singing (such as it is), I never can compose for it. My way is: I consider the poetic sentiment
correspondent to my idea of the musical expression; then
choose my theme; begin one stanza; when that is composed,
which is generally the most difficult part of the business,
I walk out, sit down now and then, look out for subjects
in nature around me that are in unison and harmony with
the cogitations of my fancy, and workings of my bosom;
humming every now and then the air with the verses
I have framed. When I feel my Muse beginning to jade, I
retire to the solitary fireside of my study, and there commit
my effusions to paper; swinging at intervals on the hind-
legs of my elbow chair, by way of calling forth my own
critical strictures as my pen goes on. Seriously, this, at

home, is almost invariably my way. What damn'd
egotism!

—*Robert Burns*

From "Mrs. Browning's Life, Letters and Essays."

Oh—you are a gnasher of teeth in criticism, I see!—
you are a lion and a tiger in one, and in a most carnivorous
mood, over and above. My dear Mr. Horne, do you know,
I could not help, in the midst of my horror and Pan-ic
terror, smiling outright at the naïveté of your doubt as
to whether my rhymes were really meant for rhymes at
all? That is the naïveté of a right savage nature—of an
Indian playing with a tomahawk, and speculating as to
whether the white faces had any feeling in their skulls,
quand même! Know, then, that my rhymes *are* really
meant for rhymes—and that I take them to be actual
rhymes—as good rhymes as any used by rhymers, and that
in no spirit of carelessness or easy writing, or desire to
escape difficulties, have I run into them,—but 'chosen
them, selected them, on principle, and with the determinate
purpose of doing my best, in and out of this poem, to have
them received! What you say of a "poet's duty," no
one in the world can feel more deeply, in the verity of
it, than myself. If I fail ultimately before the public—
that is, before the people—for an ephemeral popularity
does not appear to me worth trying for—it will not be
because I have shrunk from the amount of labor—where
labor could do anything. I have *worked* at poetry—it has
not been with me revery, but art. As the physician and
lawyer work at their several professions, so have I, and so

do I, apply to mine. And this I say, only to put by any charge of carelessness which may rise up to the verge of your lips or thoughts.

—*Elizabeth Barrett Browning*

From "The Letters of Elizabeth Barrett Browning," by Kenyon. To H. S. Boyd.

. . . Oh, and I think I told you, when giving you the history of "Lady Geraldine's Courtship," that I wrote the *thirteen* last pages of it in one day. I ought to have said *nineteen* pages instead. But don't tell anybody; only keep the circumstance in your mind when you need it and see the faults. Nobody knows of it except you and Mr. Kenyon and my own family for the reason I told you. I sent off that poem to the press piece-meal, as I never in my life did before with any poem. And since I wrote to you I have heard of Mr. Eagles, one of the first writers in "Blackwoods" and a man of very refined taste, adding another name to the many of those who have preferred it to anything in the two volumes. He says he has read it at least six times aloud to various persons, and calls it a "beautiful *sui generis* drama." On which Mr. Kenyon observes that I am "ruined for life, and shall be sure never to take pains with any poem again." . . .

—*Elizabeth Barrett Browning.*

From "Mrs. Browning's Life, Letters and Essays."

Mr. Wordsworth began his day with a dignity and determination of purpose which might well have startled the public and all its small poets and critics, his natural enemies. He laid down fixed principles in his prefaces, and carried them out with rigid boldness in his poems; and when the world laughed, he bore it well. With a severe hand he tore away from his art the encumbering artifices of his predecessors, and he walked upon the pride of criticism with greater pride. He laid his hand upon the Pegasean mane, and testified that it was not floss-silk. He testified that the ground was not all lawn or bowling-green, and that the forest trees were not clipped upon a pattern. He scorned to be contented with a tradition of beauty, or with an abstraction of the beautiful. He refused to work, as others had done, like those sculptors who make all their noses in the fashion of that of the Medicean Venus, until no one has his own nose, Nature being "cut to order." . . .

—Elizabeth Barrett Browning.

From "Biographia Literaria."

. . . With no other privilege than that of sympathy and sincere good wishes, I would address an affectionate exhortation to the youthful *literati*, grounded on my own experience. It will be but short; for the beginning, middle, and end converge to one charge: *never pursue literature as a trade*. With the exception of one extraordinary man, I have never known an individual, least of all an individual of genius, healthy or happy without a *profession*, that is, some *regular* employment, which does not depend on the will of the moment, and which can be carried out so far *mechanically* that an average *quantum* only of health, spirits, and intellectual exertion are requisite to its faithful discharge. Three hours of leisure, unannoyed by any alien anxiety, and looked forward to with delight as a change and recreation, will suffice to realize in literature a larger product of what is truly genial, than weeks of compulsion. Money and immediate reputation form only an arbitrary and accidental end of literary labor. The hope of increasing them by any given exertion will often prove a stimulant to industry; but the necessity of acquiring them will in all works of genius convert the stimulant into a narcotic. Motives by excess reverse their very nature, and instead of exciting, stun and stupify the mind.

—*Samuel Taylor Coleridge*

From "Life, Letters and Literary Remains of John Keats." To Reynolds.

. . . It may be said that we ought to read our contemporaries, that Wordsworth, etc., should have their due from us. But, for the sake of a few fine imaginative or domestic passages, are we to be bullied into a certain philosophy engendered in the whims of an egotist? Every man has his speculations, but every man does not brood and peacock over them till he makes a false coinage and deceives himself. Many a man can travel to the very bourne of Heaven, and yet want confidence to put down his half-seeing. Sancho will invent a journey heaven-ward as well as anybody. We hate poetry that has a palpable design upon us, and if we do not agree, seems to put its hand into its breeches pocket. Poetry should be great and unobtrusive, a thing which enters into one's soul, and does not startle it or amaze it with itself, but with its subject. How beautiful are the retired flowers! How would they lose their beauty were they to throng into the highway, crying out, "Admire me, I am a violet! Dote upon me, I am a primrose!" Modern poets differ from the Elizabethans in this: each of the moderns, like an Elector of Hanover, governs his petty state, and knows how many straws are swept daily from the causeways in all his dominions, and has a continual itching that all the housewives should have their coppers well scoured. The ancients were Emperors of vast provinces; they had only heard of the remote ones, and scarcely cared to visit them. I will cut all this. I will have no more of Wordsworth or Hunt in particular. Why should we be of the tribe of Manasseh, when we can wander with Esau? Why should we kick against the pricks when we can walk on roses? Why should we be owls, when we can be eagles? Why be teased with "nice-eyed wagtails," when we have in sight "the cherub Contemplation"? Why with Wordsworth's "Matthew with a bough of wilding in his hand," when we can have Jacques "under an oak," etc.? The secret of the "bough of wilding" will run through your head faster than I can write it.

—*John Keats*

From "Sir Walter Scott as a Critic of Literature."

. . . "To confess to you the truth," says the "Author" in the introductory Epistle, to *Nigel*, "the works and passages in which I have succeeded, have uniformly been written with the greatest rapidity; and when I have seen some of these placed in opposition with others, and commended as more highly finished, I could appeal to pen and standish, that the parts in which I have come feebly off were by much the more laboured." He attempted to write *Rokeby* with great care, but threw the first version into the fire because he concluded that he had "corrected the spirit out of it, as a lively pupil is sometimes flogged into a dunce by a severe schoolmaster." He was better satisfied with the result when he resumed his pen in his "old Cossack manner." Similarly he wrote of John Home's tragedy, *Douglas,* that the finest scene was, "we learn with pleasure but without surprise," unchanged from the first draft; and elsewhere he speaks of the greater chance for popularity of the "bold, decisive, but light-touched strain of poetry or narrative in literary composition," over the "more highly-wrought performance."

*　　*　　*　　*　　*　　*

Scott practically never rewrote his prose, and the result gave Hazlitt opportunity to say: "We should think the writer could not possibly read the manuscript after he has once written it, or overlook the press." His habit of carrying two trains of thought on together was also responsible for slips in diction and syntax. An amanuensis working for him noticed this peculiarity, and Scott said in his *Journal*: "There must be two currents of ideas going on in my mind at the same time. . . . I always laugh when I hear people say, Do one thing at once. I have done a dozen things at once all my life."

But the making of poetry required more attention. "Verse I write twice, and sometimes three times over," he said, and one is moved to wonder whether the distaste for writing poetry, that he professed about 1822, arose largely from a growing aversion to what he probably considered extreme care in composition. A series of three comments on his own poetry may be given to illustrate his widely varying moods in regard to it. They are all taken from letters written not far from the time when *Marmion* was published. "As for poetry, it is very little labour to me; indeed 'twere pity of my life should I spend much time on the light and loose sort of poetry which alone I can pretend to write." "I believe no man now alive writes more rapidly than I do (no great recommendation), but I never think of making verses till I have a sufficient stock of poetical ideas to supply them." "If I ever write another poem, I am determined to make every single couplet of it as perfect as my uttermost care and attention can possibly effect." In spite of this momentary resolution to take more pains with his next poem, he was unable to do so when the time came; or if, as in the case of *Rokeby* he did make the attempt, the results seemed to him unsatisfactory. Yet verse required much more careful finishing than prose, even when it was written by Scott, and this fact has been too little emphasized in discussions of his transition from verse to prose romances.

From "Tennyson: A Memoir." A letter to Dawson of Montreal.

Your explanatory notes are very much to the purpose, and I do not object to your finding parallelisms. They

must always occur. A man (a Chinese scholar) some time
ago wrote to me saying that in an unknown, untranslated
Chinese poem there were two whole lines of mine almost
word for word. Why not? Are not human eyes all over
the world looking at the same objects, and must there not
consequently be coincidences of thought and impressions
and expressions? It is scarcely possible for anyone to
say or write anything in this late time of the world to
which, in the rest of the literature of the world, a parallel
could not somewhere be found. But when you say that
this passage or that was suggested by Wordsworth or
Shelley or another, I demur; and more, I wholly disagree.
There was a period in my life when, as an artist, Turner
for instance, takes rough sketches of landskip, etc., in
order to work them eventually into some great picture,
so I was in the habit of chronicling, in four or five words
or more, whatever might strike me as picturesque in
Nature. I never put these down, and many and many a
line has gone away on the north wind, but some remain:
e.g.

A full sea glazed with muffled moonlight.

Suggestion

The sea one night at Torquay, when Torquay was the
most lovely sea-village in England, tho' now a smoky town.
The sky was covered with thin vapour, and the moon behind it.

A great black cloud
Drags inward from the deep.

Suggestion

A coming storm seen from the top of Snowdon.
In the "Idylls of the King,"

> With all
> Its stormy crests that smote against the skies.

Suggestion

A storm which came upon us in the middle of the North Sea
As the water-lily starts and slides.

Suggestion

Water-lilies in my own pond, seen on a gusty day with my own eyes. They did start and slide in the sudden puffs of wind till caught and stayed by the tether of their own stalks, quite as true as Wordsworth's simile and more in detail.

> A wild wind shook,—
> Follow, follow, thou shalt win.

Suggestion

I was walking in the New Forest. A wind did arise and
Shake the songs, the whispers and the shrieks
Of the wild wood together.

The wind I believe was a west wind, but because I wished the Prince to go south, I turned the wind to the south, and naturally the wind said "follow." I believe the resemblance which you note is just a chance one. Shelley's lines are not familiar to me tho' of course, if they occur in the Prometheus, I must have read them. I could multiply instances, but I will not bore you, and far indeed am I from asserting that books as well as Nature are not, and ought not to be suggestive to the poet. I am sure that I myself, and many others, find a peculiar charm in those passages of such great masters as Virgil or Milton where they adopt the creation of a bygone poet, and re-clothe it more or less, according to their own fancy. But there is, I fear, a prosaic set growing up among us, editors of booklets, book-worms, index-hunters, or men of great memories and no imagination, who *impute themselves* to the poet, and so believe that *he*, too, has no imagination, but is for ever poking his nose between the pages of some old volume in order to see what he can appropriate. They will not allow one to say "Ring the bell" without finding that we have taken it from Sir P. Sidney, or even to use such a simple expression as the ocean "roars," without finding out the precise verse in Homer or Horace from which we have plagiarised it (fact!).

I have known an old fish-wife, who had lost two sons at sea, clench her fist at the advancing tide on a stormy day and cry out, "Ay! roar, do! how I hates to see thee show thy white teeth." Now if I had adopted her exclamation and put it into the mouth of some old woman in one of my poems, I daresay the critics would have thought it original enough, but would most likely have advised me to go to Nature for my old women and not to my own imagination, and indeed it is a strong figure.

Here is another anecdote about suggestion. When I was about twenty or twenty-one I went on a tour to the Pyrenees. Lying among these mountains before a water-fall that comes down one thousand or twelve hundred feet I sketched it (according to my custom then) in these words:

Slow-dropping veils of thinnest lawn.

When I printed this, a critic informed me that "lawn"

was the material used in theatres to imitate a waterfall, and graciously added, "Mr. T. should not go to the boards of a theatre but to Nature herself for his suggestions." And I had gone to Nature herself.

I think it is a moot point whether, if I had known how that effect was produced on the stage, I should have ventured to publish the line.

I find that I have written, quite contrary to my custom, a letter, when I had merely intended to thank you for your interesting commentary.

Thanking you again for it, I beg you to believe me

Very faithfully yours,

—A. Tennyson

SPECIMENS OF REVISIONS

From "In Memoriam, The Princess, Maud," by Tennyson. Edited by J. C. Collins. This song was added in 1850, but the fourth and thirteenth line were added in 1851; lines 6-9 inclusive were omitted after 1850 and not reinserted till 1867.

As thro' the land at eve we went,
    And pluck'd the ripen'd ears,
We fell out, my wife and I,
O we fell out I know not why,
    And kiss'd again with tears.
And blessings on the falling out
    That all the more endears,
When we fall out with those we love
    And kiss again with tears!

For when we came where lies the child
  We lost in other years,
There above the little grave,
O there above the little grave,
  We kiss'd again with tears.

—*Edited by J. C. Collins*

From "The Poetical Works of William Blake." Edited by Sampson.

THE TIGER

Tiger! Tiger! burning bright
In the forests of the night,
What immortal hand or eye
Could frame thy fearful symmetry?

In what distant deeps or skies
Burnt the fire of thine eyes?
On what wings dare he aspire?
What the hand dare seize the fire?

And what shoulder, and what art,
Could twist the sinews of thy heart?
And when thy heart began to beat,
What dread hand? and what dread feet?

What the hammer? what the chain?
In what furnace was thy brain?
What the anvil? what dread grasp
Dare its deadly terrors clasp?

When the stars threw down their spears,
And water'd heaven with their tears,
Did he smile his work to see?
Did he who made the Lamb make thee?

Tiger! Tiger! burning bright
In the forests of the night,
What immortal hand or eye,
Dare frame thy fearful symmetry?

The original draft of "The Tiger," written upon two
opposite pages of the *Rosetti MS.*, enables us to follow every
step in the composition of the poem. On the left-hand
page is found the first rough cast of stanzas i, ii, iii, iv, and
vi. In stanza iii the manuscript version throws light upon
a verse which has proved a crux to many of Blake's readers
and commentators. It will be seen from the appended
transcript that Blake at first intended the line

"What dread hand and what dread feet"

as the beginning of a sentence running on into the next
quatrain. Dissatisfied with the form of this unfinished
stanza, he cancelled it altogether, leaving the preceding
line as it stood; but subsequently, when engraving the
poem for the *Songs of Experience*, converted the passage, by a change of punctuation, into its present shape:

"What dread hand? & what dread feet?"

a line exactly parallel in form to

"What the hammer? what the chain?"

of the following stanza. We have yet another reading in

Dr. Malkin's *Father's Memoirs of His Child* (1806), where the version of "The Tiger," presumably supplied to the author by Blake himself, contains the variant

"What dread hand forged thy dread feet?"

On the opposite page of the *MS. Book* is the first draft of stanza v, and above it, though probably written after, a revised version of ii, which differs from that finally adopted. To the right of these two stanzas follows a fair copy of i, iii, v, and vi, which, except for unimportant differences of capitalization, and the readings "dare frame" for "could frame" in the first, and "hand and eye" for "hand or eye" in the first and last stanzas, is identical with the text of the engraved *Songs*.

The following is a faithful transcript of the original draft of "The Tiger" in the *MS.*, Blake's variant readings being indicated typographically by placing them in consecutive order, one below another, deleted words or lines being printed in italics. The manuscript is unpunctuated throughout.

THE TYGER

Tyger Tyger burning bright
In the forests of the night
What immortal hand & eye

or

Could frame thy fearful symmetry
Dare

In what distant deeps or skies
Burnt in
Burnt the fire of thine eyes
The cruel
On what wings dare he aspire
What the hand dare seize the fire

And what shoulder & what art
Could twist the sinews of thy heart
And when thy heart began to beat
What dread hand & what dread feet
Could fetch it from the furnace deep
And in thy horrid ribs dare steep
In the well of sanguine woe
In what clay & in what mould
Were thy eyes of fury rolld

What the hammer *what* the chain
Where *where*
In what furnace was thy brain
What the anvil What *the arm*
arm
grasp
clasp
dread grasp
Could its deadly terrors *clasp*
Dare *grasp*
clasp

Tyger Tyger burning bright
In the forests of the night

What immortal hand & eye
Dare *form* thy fearful symmetry
        frame
[*On the opposite page*]
Burnt in distant deeps or skies
The cruel fire of thine eyes
Could heart descend or wings aspire
What the hand dare seize the fire

3 And *did he laugh* his work to see
        dare he *smile*
                laugh
What the shoulder   what the knee
        ankle
4 *Did* he who made the lamb make thee
  Dare
1 When the stars threw down their spears
2 And waterd heaven with their tears

From "Works of Cowper." To the Rev. John Newton.

. . . Having never in my life perused a page of Aristotle, I am glad to have had an opportunity of learning more than (I suppose) he would have taught me, from the writings of two modern critics. I felt myself too a little disposed to compliment my own acumen upon the occasion. For, though the art of writing and composing was never much my study, I did not find that they had any great news to tell me. They have assisted me in putting my observations into some method, but have not suggested many of which I was not by some means or other previously apprized. In fact, critics did not originally beget authors, but authors made critics. Common sense dictated to writers the necessity of method, connexion, and thoughts congruous to the nature of their subject; genius prompted them with embellishments, and then came the critics. Observing the good effects of an attention to these items, they enacted laws for the observance of them in time to come, and, having drawn their rules for good writing from what was actually well written, boasted themselves the inventors of an art which yet the authors of the day had already exemplified. They are, however, useful in their way, giving us at one view a map of the boundaries which propriety sets to fancy, and serving as judges to whom the public may at once appeal, when pestered with the vagaries of those who have had the hardiness to transgress them.

—*William Cowper*

From "Works of Cowper." To the Rev. William Unwin.

MY DEAR WILLIAM: A poet can but ill spare time for prose. The truth is, I am in haste to finish my transcript, that you may receive it time enough to give it a leisurely reading before you go to town; which, whether I shall be able to accomplish, is at present uncertain. I have the whole punctuation to settle, which in blank verse is of the last importance, and of a species peculiar to that composition; for I know no use of points, unless to direct the voice, the management of which, in the reading of blank verse, being more difficult than in the reading of any other poetry, requires perpetual hints and notices to regulate the inflexions, cadences, and pauses. This, however, is an affair that, in spite of grammarians, must be left pretty much *ad libitum scriptoris.* . . .

—*William Cowper*

From "Works of Cowper." To Joseph Hill.

MY DEAR FRIEND: I write in a nook that I call my *boudoir*. It is a summer-house not much bigger than a sedan-chair, the door of which opens into the garden, that is now crowded with pinks, roses, and honeysuckles, and the window into my neighbour's orchard. It formerly served an apothecary, now dead, as a smoking-room; and under my feet is a trap-door which once covered a hole in the ground, where he kept his bottles; at present, however, it is dedicated to sublimer uses. Having lined it with garden-mats, and furnished it with a table and two chairs, here I write all that I write in summer time, whether to my friends or to the public. It is secure from all noise, and a refuge from all intrusion; for intruders sometimes trouble me in the winter evenings at Olney: but (thanks to my *boudoir!*) I can now hide myself from them. A poet's retreat is sacred; they acknowledge the truth of that proposition, and never presume to violate it.

—*William Cowper*

From "Pope's Works." To Walsh.

I cannot omit the first opportunity of making you my acknowledgments for reviewing those papers of mine. You have no less right to correct me, than the same hand that raised a tree has to prune it. I am convinced, as well as you, that one may correct too much; for in poetry, as in painting, a man may lay colours one upon another till they stiffen and deaden the piece. Besides, to bestow heightening on every part is monstrous: some parts ought to be lower than the rest; and nothing looks more ridiculous than a work where the thoughts, however different in their own nature, seem all on a level: it is like a meadow newly mown, where weeds, grass, and flowers are all laid even, and appear undistinguished. I believe, too, that sometimes our first thoughts are the best, as the first squeezing of the grapes makes the finest and richest wine.

I have not attempted anything of a pastoral comedy, because I think the taste of our age will not relish a poem of that sort. People seek for what they call wit, on all subjects, and in all places; not considering that nature loves truth so well, that it hardly ever admits of flourishing. Conceit is to nature what paint is to beauty; it is not only needless, but impairs what it would improve. There is a certain majesty in simplicity, which is far above all the quaintness of wit; insomuch that the critics have excluded wit from the loftiest poetry, as well as the lowest, and forbid it to the epic no less than the pastoral. . . .

—*Alexander Pope*

From Spence's "Anecdotes of Books and Men."

The things that I have written fastest, have always pleased the most.—I wrote the Essay on Criticism fast; for I had digested all the matter in prose, before I began upon it in verse. The Rape of the Lock was written fast: all the machinery was added afterwards; and the making that, and what was published before, hit so well together, is, I think, one of the greatest proofs of judgment of anything I ever did. I wrote most of the Iliad fast; a great deal of it on journeys, from the little pocket Homer on that shelf there; and often forty or fifty verses in a morning in bed.—The Dunciad cost me as much pains as anything I ever wrote.

—*Alexander Pope*

We should manage our thoughts in composing a poem as shepherds do their flowers in making a garland; first select the choicest, and then dispose them in the most proper places, where they give a luster to each other: like the feathers in Indian crowns, which are so managed that every one reflects a part of its color and gloss on the next.

—*Alexander Pope*

From "The Crystal."

> Ye companies of governor-spirits grave,
> Bards, and old bringers-down of flaming news
> From steep-wall'd heavens, holy malcontents,
> Sweet seers, and stellar visionaries, all
> That brood about the skies of poesy,
> Full bright ye shine, insuperable stars;
> Yet, if a man look hard upon you, none
> With total lustre blazeth, no, not one
> But hath some heinous freckle of the flesh

Upon his shining cheek, not one but winks
His ray, opaqued with intermittent mist
Of defect; yea, you masters all must ask
Some sweet forgiveness, which we leap to give,
We lovers of you, heavenly-glad to meet
Your largesse so with love, and interplight
Your geniuses with our mortalities.

—*Sidney Lanier*

From "Discoveries."

There is a sentence in *The Marriage of Heaven and Hell*
that is meaningless until we understand Blake's system
of correspondences. "The best wine is the oldest, the
best water the newest." Water is experience, immediate
sensation, and wine is emotion, and it is with the intellect,
as distinguished from imagination, that we enlarge the
bounds of experience and separate it from all but itself,
from illusion, from memory, and create among other things
science and good journalism. Emotion, on the other hand,
grows intoxicating and delightful after it has been en-
riched with the memory of old emotions, with all the
uncounted flavours of old experience; and it is necessarily
some antiquity of thought, emotions that have been deep-
ened by the experiences of many men of genius, that dis-
tinguishes the cultivated man. The subject matter of
his meditation and invention is old, and he will disdain
a too conscious originality in the arts as in those matters
of daily life where, is it not Balzac who says, "we are
all conservatives"? He is above all things well-bred, and
whether he write or paint will not desire a technique that

denies or obtrudes his long and noble descent. Corneille and Racine did not deny their masters, and when Dante spoke of his master Virgil there was no crowing of the cock.

—*William Butler Yeats*

From "Poetry and Tradition."

> Him who trembles before the flame and the flood,
> And the winds that blow through the starry ways;
> Let the starry winds and the flame and the flood
> Cover over and hide, for he has no part
> With the proud, majestical multitude.

Three types of men have made all beautiful things. Aristocracies have made beautiful manners, because their place in the world puts them above the fear of life, and the countrymen have made beautiful stories and beliefs, because they have nothing to lose and so do not fear, and the artists have made all the rest, because Providence has filled them with recklessness. All these look backward to a long tradition, for, being without fear, they have held to whatever pleased them.

—*William Butler Yeats*

John Gould Fletcher's "Thoughts on the Making of Poetry."

Poetry is always born out of a state of conflict between the poet's inner aspiration and his outer knowledge and perception of reality. The inner aspiration of the poet may be unconscious, and the outer knowledge conscious, or vice versa; but one or the other is always unconscious, and it is out of the fusion of the poet's consciousness with his sub-consciousness that the poem comes to him. The interest, therefore, of any fairly good and complete body of poetry is that it reveals not only the influence of the poet's own times, but the manner of working which his mind has; and the study of poetry may be fairly undertaken not only as a means of affording us touchstones of rhythmic and verbal beauty; but also as a not-unprofitable branch of human history and psychology.

My own method of writing poetry is as follows: Something which I have seen, heard, or experienced in life affects me very strongly. I brood upon it, largely unconsciously, until suddenly, for no apparent reason, a line or a group of lines form themselves in my brain, in some way connected with the subject on which I have been thinking. These lines are not necessarily the opening lines of the poem; they may be its refrain, or leading idea, but when they have established themselves in my memory for the time being, other lines are added to them. In this way I have often composed as many as a dozen lines of poetry before putting pen to paper. When I finally sit down to the actual task of composition, I generally (except in the case of a very long poem, of which the process of incubation has gone on for a considerable time) write out the whole poem in a single draft and at a single sitting, my aim being to preserve my original subconscious impulse as long as possible.

This original draft may later be amplified or corrected, but never entirely rewritten. During the first heat of composition, I find that I am usually so entirely absorbed in the subject as to be oblivious of the flight of time, and sometimes I am so completely unaware of what it is that I am putting on paper, that it is only at a later reading that

I recognize its value. This seems to be a fairly common experience with most poets; and I should say that the great point about the first draft of any poem is to be able to stop before exhaustion has set in, and also to be able to look upon it later with a detached and refreshed mind. Sometimes the subconscious discovery I have made in writing a poem urges me to compose a number of others on similar or related lines. In this way I wrote my colour-symphonies, and a great many poems contained in "The Tree of Life." But there is a danger in thus amplifying upon the basis of a single impulse, unless the impulse be of such magnitude and quality as to affect the whole of the poet's after-life, such as the impulse from which sprang "The Divine Comedy" or "Leaves of Grass."

Frequently I have noticed that it is not a single impulse that has produced in me a poem, but the fusion of several. Thus, for example, my poem on "Lincoln" came into being, first, because I had been strongly moved by reading Herndon's Life; second, because I had but recently spent a summer in the pine woods of Michigan, and had been powerfully affected by the backwoods atmosphere in which Lincoln had grown to manhood; third, because of the troubled political situation in America, in the spring of 1916, when the poem was actually composed. Incidentally, I may also remark that this poem was written in a single afternoon, but that my mind had in some way been preparing for it for nearly a year before. And in much the same way I might analyse many of my longer and better-known poems.

As regards the vexed question of the dividing line between prose and poetry and where it ought to be drawn, I should like to say that poetry differs from prose largely in a more complete simplification of detail and of rhythm. The more full, rich and detailed poetry and prose are, the nearer do they approach each other. In nothing was Shakespeare greater than in his ability to turn from magnificent poetry to superb prose. "Free verse," rightly understood as verse that permits the greatest amount of individual variation in metrical technique, as well as strongly rhythmed prose, are attempts, more or less satisfactory, to bridge over the gap that separates poetry from prose.

I find that the practice of most poets differs very widely in regard to rewriting and revision. I never do more than two or three drafts of any poem; but I know of another poet who has admitted to as many as twenty. But I have sometimes sketched out an idea for a poem, found my first draft unsatisfactory, torn it up, and discovered the selfsame idea in another guise, presenting itself to me later. In this respect I think it is a mistake to assume that poets are necessarily short-winded or short-lived. If Keats and Shelley had lived longer, and if the public had responded more generously to their work, we might have had more dramas on the lines of "The Cenci" and "Hyperion" would have been more than a fragment. The short-winded poet is always the poet incapable of drawing much profit from added experience, and inclined to lose himself in a realm of pure fantasy. Examples of such poets are Coleridge and Poe.

On the subject of the poetic vocabulary, and how far this approximates or diverges from that of prose, I feel inclined to be cautious. Prose, in general, is a medium

permitting of more variety in handling than poetry; therefore, the vocabulary of almost any prose, except the baldest
and most restrained narrative, is certain to contain more
divergent elements than almost any poetry. Where the
prose-writer seeks for diversity, the poet aims at concentration. This concentration can only be gained by adopt-
ing a very definite attitude of acceptance to the type of
word that seems to convey most fully the quality of one's
own intellectual and emotional reactions, and by studying
the work of those poets whose work is most sympathetic. The
poet in general should strive to steer, if possible, a midway
course between realism and fantasy; the highest poetry
in the world always contains both, welded together and
transmuted into unforgettable music.

—John Gould Fletcher

Sara Teasdale's Theory.

My theory is that poems are written because of a state
of emotional irritation. It may be present for some time
before the poet is conscious of what is tormenting him.
The emotional irritation springs, probably, from subconscious combinations of partly forgotten thoughts and feelings. Coming together, like electrical currents in a thunder storm, they produce a poem. A poem springs from
emotions produced by an actual experience, or almost as
forcefully, from those produced by an imaginary experience. In either case, the poem is written to free the poet
from an emotional burden.

Out of the fog of emotional restlessness from which a

poem springs, the basic idea emerges sometimes slowly, sometimes in a flash. This idea is known at once to be the light toward which the poet was groping. He now walks round and round it, so to speak, looking at it from all sides, trying to see which aspect of it is the most vivid. When he has hit upon what he believes is his peculiar angle of vision, the poem is fairly begun. The first line comes floating toward him with a charming definiteness of color and music. In my own case, the poems being brief, the rhythm usually follows, in a more general way, the rhythm of the first line. The more swiftly the poem forms itself, the better it is likely to be. This does not mean that a polishing process may not be long and sometimes disheartening.

Brief lyrical poems are usually moulded in the poet's mind. They are far more fluid before they touch ink and paper than they ever are afterward. The warmth of the idea that generated the poem should vary the music and make the verses clear, ductile, a finished whole, before they touch cold white paper. In the process of moulding his idea the poet will be at white heat of intellectual and emotional activity, bearing in mind that every word, every syllable, must be an unobtrusive and yet an indispensable part of his creation. Every beat of his rhythm, the color of each word, the ring of each rhyme, must conform inevitably to his feeling. By shaping his poem with perfect exactitude to hold his emotion, he fulfills his subconscious aim in its composition. He sets himself free by pouring his thought into a form which holds it completely, and in which he can contemplate it as a thing apart from himself.

—Sara Teasdale

Amy Lowell on "The Process of Making Poetry."

In answering the question, How are poets made? my instinctive answer is a flat "I don't know." It makes not the slightest difference that the question as asked me refers solely to my own poems, for I know as little of how they are made as I do of any one else's. What I do know about them is only a millionth part of what there must be to know. I meet them where they touch consciousness, and that is already a considerable distance along the road of evolution.

Whether poetry is the fusion of contradictory ideas, as Mr. Graves believes, or the result and relief of emotional irritation and tension, as Sara Teasdale puts it, or the yielding to a psychical state verging on daydream, as Professor Prescott has written a whole book to prove, it is impossible for anyone to state definitely. All I can confidently assert from my own experience is that it is not daydream, but an entirely different psychic state and one peculiar to itself.

The truth is that there is a little mystery here, and no one is more conscious of it than the poet himself. Let us admit at once that a poet is something like a radio aërial— he is capable of receiving messages on waves of some sort; but he is more than an aërial, for he possesses the capacity of transmuting these messages into those patterns of words we call poems.

It would seem that a scientific definition of a poet might put it something like this: a man of an extraordinarily sensitive and active subconscious personality, fed by, and feeding, a non-resistant consciousness. A common phrase among poets is, "It came to me." So hackneyed has this

become that one learns to suppress the expression with
care, but really it is the best description I know of the
conscious arrival of a poem.

Sometimes the external stimulus which has produced a
poem is known or can be traced. It may be a sight, a
sound, a thought, or an emotion. Sometimes the consciousness has no record of the initial impulse, which has either
been forgotten or springs from a deep, unrealized memory.
But whatever it is, emotion, apprehended or hidden, is a
part of it, for only emotion can rouse the subconscious
into action. How carefully and precisely the subconscious
mind functions, I have often been a witness to in my own
work. An idea will come into my head for no apparent
reason; "The Bronze Horses," for instance. I registered
the horses as a good subject for a poem; and, having so
registered them, I consciously thought no more about the
matter. But what I had really done was to drop my subject into the subconscious, much as one drops a letter into
the mail-box. Six months later, the words of the poem
began to come into my head, the poem—to use my private
vocabulary—was "there."

Some poets speak of hearing a voice speaking to them,
and say that they write almost to dictation. I do not
know whether my early scientific training is responsible
for my using a less picturesque vocabulary, or whether their
process really differs from mine. I do not hear a voice,
but I do hear words pronounced, only the pronouncing
is toneless. The words seem to be pronounced in my head,
but with nobody speaking them. This is an effect with
which I am familiar, for I always *hear* words even when I
am reading to myself, and still more when I am writing.

In writing, I frequently stop to read aloud what I have written, although this is really hardly necessary so clearly do the words sound in my head.

The subconscious is, however, a most temperamental ally. Often he will strike work at some critical point and not another word is to be got out of him. Here is where the conscious training of the poet comes in, for he must fill in what the subconscious has left, and fill it in as much in the key of the rest as possible. Every long poem is sprinkled with these *lacunæ,* hence the innumerable re-writings which most poems undergo. Sometimes the sly subconscious partner will take pity on the struggling poet and return to his assistance, sometimes he will have nothing to do with that particular passage again. This is the reason that a poet must be both born and made. He must be born with a subconscious factory always working for him or he never can be a poet at all, and he must have knowledge and talent enough to "putty" up his holes—to use Mr. Graves's expression. Let no one undervalue this process of puttying, it is a condition of good poetry. Of the many first manuscript drafts of great poets that have passed through my hands in the last twenty-five years, I have seen none without its share of putty, and the one of all most worked over is Keats's "The Eve of St. Agnes."

Long poems are apt to take months preparing in the subconscious mind; in the case of short poems, the period of subconscious gestation may be a day or an instant, or any time between. Suddenly words are there, and there with an imperious insistence which brooks no delay. They must be written down immediately or an acute suffering comes on, a distress almost physical, which is not relieved until the poem is given right of way. I never deny poems when they come; whatever I am doing, whatever I am writing, I lay it aside and attend to the arriving poem. I am so constituted that poems seldom come when I am out of doors, or actively engaged in company. But when I am alone, an idea contingent upon something I have seen or done when I am out will announce itself, quite as though it had been biding its time until it had me quiescent and receptive.

I seldom compose in my head. The first thing I do when I am conscious of the coming of a poem is to seek paper and pencil. It seems as though the simple gazing at a piece of blank paper hypnotized me into an awareness of the subconscious. For the same reason, I seldom correct poems while walking or driving. I find that the concentration needed for this is in the nature of trance (although that is too exaggerated a word for it), and must not be broken into by considerations of where I am going or what station I am to get out at.

This state of semi-trance is not surprising when we think of short poems; what is curious is that the trancelike state can hold over interruptions in the case of long poems. When a poem is so long that days or weeks are needed to write it, the mere sitting down to continue it produces the requisite frame of mind, which holds (except for the *lacunæ* I have spoken of) throughout its correction. On the other hand, no power will induce it if the subconscious is not ready, hence the sterile periods known to all poets.

I do believe that a poet should know all he can. No subject is alien to him, and the profounder his knowledge in any direction, the more depth will there be to his poetry.

I believe he should be thoroughly grounded in both the old and the new poetic forms, but I am firmly convinced that he must never respect tradition above his intuitive self. Let him be sure of his own sincerity above all, let him bow to no public acclaim, however alluring, and then let him write with all courage what his subconscious mind suggests to him.

—Amy Lowell

Technique, which should have been a thing absorbed so soundlessly from wide reading that you do not know it for what it is, cannot be taught in ten lessons so that you can go out and be as good a poet as if you had learned it by loving wonderfully made poems. In poetry, as in most other things, love is the fulfilling of the law. The ignorant poet may yet be a true poet. But is it not a pity that he or she should be ignorant and consider that limitation a help? For the original mind was never yet fettered by a love of learning.

—Margaret Widdemer

Sidney Lanier was of the belief that a poet should have sound scientific knowledge, should know biology, geology, archæology as well as etymology. I should add psychology, sociology, and all the other ologies there are. This is almost ridiculous, you say. There is nothing ridiculous about it. A poet should swallow the encyclopædia, and then after that the dictionary. He should be a linguist if possible. He should be a business man. He should be able to meet any type of man on his own ground and understand what he is talking about. The poet should be able, also, to relate the thing discussed to the cosmos in general as the highly specialized individual is not able to relate it. A poet should know history inside and out and should take as much interest in the days of Nebuchadnezzar as in the days of Pierpont Morgan.

—*William Rose Benét*

The sense of rhythm is the most active of my senses in relation to poetic composition. All my "Songs of the Coast Dwellers" came into my thought first as rhythm, as if I were listening to a song without words played on a violin. Then on the beat of the rhythm came the ideas and the words. There is nothing mystic nor subconscious about this. My temperament is appealed to more acutely by rhythm than by color—the rhythmic contours of a landscape mean more to me than its hues.

—*Constance Lindsay Skinner*

PERSISTENCY OF POETRY

Though the Muse be gone away,
Though she move not earth to-day,
Souls, erewhile who caught her word,
Ah! still harp on what they heard.

—*Matthew Arnold*

Who walks with Beauty has no need of fear,
The sun and moon and stars keep pace with him.

—*David Morton*

CONCERNING FAME

When Chatterton was a boy (if that uncanny little elf ever really was a boy), a china maker offered to decorate a cup especially for him. "Paint me," the child said, "paint me an angel with wings and a trumpet to trumpet my name over all the world." The anecdote provides a complete symbolism for our thought about the kind of fame that poets most desire. It must not be merely the acclaim of the vulgar; it must not be merely bellowed by radio; it must not be limited by time and space. If a poet desires fame in any proud way, he desires that sort which can make of one blood all nations on the earth and give them one pulse in the beating of his heart. It must be lofty, coming from the great to the great; illustrious, proclaimed in trumpet tones as battle and triumph are; timeless and spacious, passing from soul to soul and from age to endless age.

Blake went even further and, in one of his letters, claimed to have no care about terrestrial immortality because his work, he said, was "famed in Heaven" and "the delight of archangels." As a religious visionary he doubtless found it easy to believe that, if angels could rejoice in repentant sinners, they might also find delight in an exuberant poet. Before we can be sure that he was wrong we shall have to extend our acquaintance with angels. But we do not need to extend our acquaintance with poets in order to know that whenever they believe in angels, they probably believe in them as beings who ought to be interested in their poems. Blake was exceptional only in two ways—he had more faith in angels than most of us and his work was more deserving of their attention. What poet has not dreamed dreams somewhat like that of Jacob's about the sun and moon and stars? And, after all, why should anybody be content with fame on one poor little oblate spheroid if he believes that he is chanting before a solar system?

"It is as great a spite to be praised in the wrong place, and by a wrong person, as can be done to a noble nature," said Ben Jonson, and all who have known the sensitivity and hauteur of the masters have felt this aspect of the truth. The large audience of the little people can confer a popularity that is eloquent enough in its own way, wrought out of their blood and sweat and tears; out of their raucous hilarity and familiar affections. Yet fame is not in their gift unless they are joined in acclamation by the little audience of the great who can add insight to eloquence. Keats seems to have felt this keenly. He says:

I have not the slightest feeling of humility towards the public, or to anything in existence but the Eternal Being, the Principle of Beauty, and the Memory of Great Men.

And again,

I feel every confidence that, if I choose, I may be a popular writer. That I will never be. . . . I equally dislike the favor of the public with the love of woman. . . . I shall now consider them (the people) as debtors to me for verses, not myself to them for admiration, which I can do without. Just so much as I am humbled by the genius above my grasp, am I exalted and look with hate and contempt upon the literary world.

To be sure, wholesome citizens may often be right in their estimates of poetry when contemporray critics, hoodwinked by their own intellectual and emotional sophistication, are wrong. But wholesome citizens wabble on their æsthetic legs and fumble with their æsthetic fingers because they do not know the reasons for their sound estimates of contemporary work. They accept leadership all too readily and choose their poets with a dumb, good-natured, uncomprehending docility just as they choose tooth paste or cereals for breakfast, believing that what is widely advertised must be good. Instead of making their own opinions on the basis of sincere likes and dislikes they tend to revert to memories of what they learned about poetry in Public School Number Three. The beauty that differs from that of the past and comes to them hot and glistening like metal from a crucible is anathema to them. They will have none of it until it has cooled in its mould.

The opinions of the contemporary literary world are also unreliable for trite and obvious reasons. It is always difficult for a critic to be judicial and relate the labors of his superlative friends and positive enemies to great works of the past by which they might be tested. It is certain, also, that if two women produced work of equal value in any period of the world's history, the more charming would get the better reviews in a world of men, not because men are unfair, but because the work of the more charming woman would be better understood through the medium of her personality. Quite as certainly, in any world at all, the living man of shy, quiet, unobtrusive genius risks being brushed aside by insouciant troubadours of the common passions. Perhaps the greatest poet of our period is now working in New York, quite unknown to the bestowers of parnassian publicity. Perhaps Conrad Aiken, Ezra Pound, Maxwell Bodenheim, and Clement Wood have missed him. Perhaps Louis Untermeyer has never heard of him. Perhaps even Amy Lowell and Herbert Gorman and I have dipped no gallant flags in salutation.

Other celebrities now "flourishing in apogee" (apologies to Mr. Robinson) may never be known to posterity at all. I do not refer to good old Eddie Guest, who worries the editors of "Poetry, A Magazine of Verse," and delights thousands who never read poetry at all and never will in this incarnation. I refer to men and women who might, with a change of heart or of mind or of both, produce poetry with sound and permanent values, but of whose work we might say with Ben Jonson,

Yet their vices have not hurt them: nay, a great many have profited; for they have been loved for nothing else. . . . But a man cannot imagine that thing so foolish or rude, but will find and enjoy an Admirer; at least a Reader or Spectator.

It is pertinent, in our time and land, to remark that such specious popularity is always the result of sensationalism, the effort of the weak to startle us into attention because they are unable to awaken in us that wonder which is the gift of the strong. As Pope said, "This ambition of surprising a reader is the true natural cause of all fustian and bombast in poetry." It is also the cause of all violence and crudity, the æsthetic poor relations of power and originality.

For all these reasons fame can be awarded only by the great, by mankind, by the ages, after conference together. Yet we need not worry. In the arts the *good* men do lives after the evil is interred with their bones. Works of wisdom and beauty live eternally because they are vitalized by the "Holy Breath" of which A. E. makes mention. As Blake tells us in his proverbs of Hell,

The hours of folly are measur'd by the clock; but of wisdom no clock can measure.

And again, as if to reassure us,

Eternity is in love with the productions of time.

If a poet's work be charged with his life, and if that life has value for the race, he is certain to share Robert Herrick's "repullulation" in the "thirtieth thousand year." Therefore when a poet begins to be nervously attentive to reviewers, when he insists on reading his work, or sending it by letter to somebody who has "arrived," when he carries a chip, or a whole forest, on his shoulder because press notices are not laudatory, one of two things is wrong. Either he secretly doubts his own ability to remake people's minds by the quiet power of his work, or else, having no faith in personal immortality and little sufficing joy in the labor of creation for its own sake, he prefers to take his wages in small change while he is present with us in the flesh. He is not willing to wait for the ample, inevitable, and everlasting returns on the investment of a life. Surely, surely, he is either fearful or greedy!

We have, then, two kinds of motives for desiring fame, and the fruits of these motives; we have the austere desire of the real Seanchan which is rewarded with fame according to the measure of the achievement, and we have the feverish urge toward quick popularity which brings the briefly glittering success of the poetaster.

At its noblest the desire for fame conjoins two other desires, or is conditioned by their coming together in one soul. I mean the desire for sympathy and the desire to let light shine before men. Over and over again the poets have confessed their need of sympathy and their joy in finding it. Also, it is everywhere implicit in their writings that they believe in their poems as offspring of the light, a gift for the world. The gift must be received that the act of creation may be complete. Fame is merely the receptive and thankful answer of mankind.

Of comment on the poet's appetite for sympathy plump volumes could be made. Let Coleridge be spokesman:

Yet they knew that to praise, as mere praise, I was characteristically, almost constitutionally indifferent. In sympathy alone I found at once nourishment and stimulus; and for sympathy alone did my heart crave . . .

In a similar vein Shelley once wrote to John and Maria Gisborne:

I am fully repaid for the painful emotions from which some verses of my poems sprang, by your sympathy and approbation—which is all the reward I expect—and as much as I desire, . . . The decision of the cause, whether or no *I* am a poet, is removed from the present time to the hour when our posterity shall assemble; but the court is a very severe one, and I fear that the verdict will be ''Guilty—death!''

And of the desire to be torch-bearers as much might be said in quotation as would make an exceedingly corpulent bible of aspirations. Never a good poet lives who does not, consciously or subconsciously, envy Prometheus.

Somewhat less noble than these motives for desiring fame is the longing for power over men's minds and hearts. It is probably instinctive, a part of the aggressive male urge to live dominantly. And it is not strange that we should find it frankly expressed by such a man as Byron:

I once wrote from the fullness of my mind and the love of fame (not as an *end,* but as a *means,* to obtain that influence over men's minds which is power in itself and in its consequences).

Still lower in the scale of evaluated motives is the desire for display of which modern psychologists make much ado. Lowest of all, probably, is the competitive motive which belongs to our instinctive pugnacity.

I call this competitive motive the lowest because it is absurd. Competition cannot exist except in kind. To be a poet of any importance at all is to be unique. A good poet draws his own audience slowly from the ages and from all the zones. He has a word to say that nobody else can say for him to them, that nobody else even wants to say in just the same way. Therefore a good poet can have superiors and inferiors, but no rivals, and to be jealous is to confess a personal inadequacy. We are sometimes told that there are poets in whom this motive for desiring fame does exist. If that be true, it must be because there is no instinct in our natures that does not occasionally bring force to bear upon the poet's will to give his gift and to know that it is rewarded with a welcome.

For this reason it is all the more necessary for the laity to remember that the high hope of winning fame, though it may strengthen the ambition to write well, is not responsible for the will to create. That will is the signature of divinity in man and his inheritance from Heaven. To make poems is a poet's doom, his destiny. Even when it is most ardently desired the longing for fame is less, I believe, than the longing for expression. Says Landor,

There is delight in singing, tho' none hear.

If I should be convinced that any particular poet desired fame more than the zest of singing, I should doubt him as the feminine aristocrat used to doubt women who wore jewels of paste in the days when she was not wearing them herself, for I should have to think that his pride must be mere vanity.

A good poet's pride is not vanity; it is the antithesis of vanity; it is even compatible with deep humility, for it is a pride in his vocation, not in himself alone; it is a liberating pride, setting him free from common preferences and cheap prejudices. Let all who would be proud poets in our day begin by being humble. To be capable of silent non-resistance when reviewers scoff is to be stronger than their strength. To maintain equanimity before a mocking, misunderstanding, or negligent public may indicate victorious staying-power. Let the poets "be secret and exult." Or let them say gently with Milton:

And what am I doing? *Growing my wings* and meditating flight; but as yet our Pegasus raises himself on
very tender pinions. Let us be lowly wise!

XIX

Devouring Time, blunt thou the lion's paws,
And make the earth devour her own sweet brood;
Pluck the keen teeth from the fierce tiger's jaws,
And burn the long-lived phœnix in her blood;
Make glad and sorry seasons as thou fleets,
And do whate'er thou wilt, swift-footed Time,
To the wide world and all her fading sweets;
But I forbid thee one most heinous crime:
O, carve not with thy hours my love's fair brow,
Nor draw no lines there with thine antique pen;
Him in thy course untainted do allow
For beauty's pattern to succeeding men.
    Yet, do thy worst, old Time: despite thy wrong,
    My love shall in my verse ever live young.

                   —*William Shakespeare*

LX

Like as the waves make towards the pebbled shore,
So do our minutes hasten to their end;
Each changing place with that which goes before,
In sequent toil all forwards do contend.
Nativity, once in the main of light,
Crawls to maturity, wherewith being crown'd,
Crooked eclipses 'gainst his glory fight,
And Time that gave doth now his gift confound.

Time doth transfix the flourish set on youth
And delves the parallels in beauty's brow,
Feeds on the rarities of nature's truth,
And nothing stands but for his scythe to mow:
 And yet to times in hope my verse shall stand,
 Praising thy word, despite his cruel hand.

—*William Shakespeare*

FAMA

From "Discoveries."

A Fame that is wounded to the world, would bee better
cured by anothers *Apologie,* then its owne: For few can
apply medicines well themselves. Besides, the man that is
once hated, both his *good,* and his *evill* deeds oppress him.
He is not easily *emergent.*

—*Ben Jonson*

CENSURA DE POETIS

From "Discoveries."

Nothing in our Age, I have observ'd, is more prepos-
terous, then the *running Iudgments* upon *Poetry,* and
Poets; when wee shall heare those things commended, and
cry'd up for the best writings, which a man would scarce
vouchsafe to wrap any wholesome drug in; hee would
never light his *Tobacco* with them. And those men almost
nam'd for *Miracles,* who yet are so vile, that if a man
should goe about, to examine, and correct them, hee
must make all they have done, but one blot. Their good
is so intangled with their bad, as forcibly one must draw

on the others death with it. A Sponge dipt in Inke will doe all:

>> . . . *Comitetur punica librum*
>> *Spongia.* . . .
>
> Et paulo post
>> *Non possunt multae, una litura potest.*

Yet their vices have not hurt them: Nay, a great many have profited; for they have beene lov'd for nothing else. And this false opinion growes strong against the best men: if once it take root with the *Ignorant*. *Cestius* in his time, was preferr'd to Cicero; so farre, as the Ignorant durst. They learn'd him without booke, and had him often in their mouthes: But a man cannot imagine that thing so foolish, or rude, but will find, and enjoy an Admirer; at least, a Reader, or *Spectator*. The Puppets are seene now in despighte of the Players: *Heath's Epigrams,* and the *Skullers Poems* have their applause. There are never wanting, that dare preferre the worst *Preachers,* the worst *Pleaders,* the worst *Poets;* not that the better have left to write, or speake better, but that they that heare them judge worse; *Non illi pejus dicunt, sed his corruptius judicant.* Nay, if it were put to the question of the Waterrimer's workes, against *Spenser's;* I doubt not, but they would find more *Suffrages;* because the most favour common vices, out of a Prerogative the vulgar have, to lose their judgments; and like that which is naught.

—Ben Jonson

From "Saadi."

>> God, Who gave to him the lyre,
>> Of all mortals the desire,
>> For all breathing men's behoof,
>> Straitly charged him, "Sit aloof;"

Annexed a warning, poets say,
To the bright premium,—
Ever when twain together play
Shall the harp be dumb.

Many may come,
But one shall sing;
Two touch the string,
The harp is dumb.
Though there come a million
Wise Saadi dwells alone.

—Ralph Waldo Emerson

THE TEST

(Musa Loquitur)

I hung my verses in the wind,
Time and tide their faults may find.
All were winnowed through and through,
Five lines lasted sound and true;
Five were smelted in a pot
Than the South more fierce and hot;
These the siroc could not melt,
Fire their fiercer flaming felt,
And the meaning was more white
Than July's meridian light.
Sunshine cannot bleach the snow
Nor time unmake what poets know.
Have you eyes to find the five
Which five hundred did survive?

—Ralph Waldo Emerson

From "Letters of Elizabeth Barrett Browning." To Ruskin.

Let me consider how to answer your questions: My poetry—which you are so good to, and which you once thought "sickly," you say, and why not? (I have often written sickly poetry, I do not doubt—I have been sickly myself!)—has been called by much harder names. . . . My friends took some trouble with me at one time; but though I am not self-willed naturally, as you will find when you know me, I never could adopt the counsel urged upon me to keep in sight always the stupidest person of my acquaintance in order to clear and judicious forms of composition. Will you set me down as arrogant, if I say that the longer I live in this writing and reading world, the more convinced I am that the mass of readers *never* receive a poet (you, who are a poet yourself, must surely observe that) without intermediation? The few understand, appreciate and distribute to the multitude below. Therefore to say a thing faintly, because saying it strongly sounds odd or obscure or unattractive for some reason, to "careless readers," does appear to me bad policy as well as bad art. Is not art, like virtue, to be practised for its own sake first? If we sacrifice our ideal to notions of immediate utility, would it not be better for us to write tracts at once?   —*Elizabeth Barrett Browning*

MEMORABILIA

Ah, did you once see Shelley plain,
    And did he stop and speak to you,
And did you speak to him again?
    How strange it seems and new!

But you were living before that,
    And also you are living after;
And the memory I started at—
    My starting moves your laughter!

I crossed a moor, with a name of its own,
    And a certain use in the world no doubt,
Yet a hand's-breadth of it shines alone
    'Mid the blank miles round about:

For there I picked up on the heather,
    And there I put inside my breast
A moulted feather, an eagle-feather!
    Well, I forget the rest.

—*Robert Browning*

POPULARITY

As the previous poem was an appreciation of Shelley,
so this, of Keats.

Stand still, true poet that you are!
    I know you; let me try and draw you.
Some night you'll fail us: when afar
    You rise, remember one man saw you,
Knew you, and named a star!

My star, God's glow-worm! Why extend
    That loving hand of his which leads you,
Yet locks you safe from end to end
    Of this dark world, unless he needs you,
Just saves your light to spend?

His clenched hand shall unclose at last,
  I know, and let out all the beauty:
My poet holds the future fast,
  Accepts the coming ages' duty,
Their present for this past.

That day, the earth's feast-master's brow
  Shall clear, to God the chalice raising;
"Others give best at first, but thou
  Forever set'st our table praising,
Keep'st the good wine till now!"

Meantime, I'll draw you as you stand,
  With few or none to watch and wonder:
I'll say—a fisher, on the sand
  By Tyre the old, with ocean-plunder,
A netful, brought to land.

Who has not heard how Tyrian shells
  Enclosed the blue, that dye of dyes
Whereof one drop worked miracles,
  And colored like Astarte's eyes
Raw silk the merchant sells?

And each bystander of them all
  Could criticise, and quote tradition
How depths of blue sublimed some pall
  —To get which, pricked a king's ambition;
Worth sceptre, crown and ball.

Yet, there's the dye, in that rough mesh,
　　The sea has only just o'er-whispered!
Live whelks, each lip's beard dripping fresh,
　　As if they still the water's lisp heard
Through foam the rock-weeds thresh.

Enough to furnish Solomon
　　Such hangings for his cedar-house,
That, when gold-robed he took the throne
　　In that abyss of blue, the Spouse
Might swear his presence shone.

Most like the centre-spike of gold
　　Which burns deep in the bluebell's womb
What time, with ardors manifold,
　　The bee goes singing to her groom,
Drunken and overbold.

Mere conchs! not fit for warp or woof!
　　Till cunning come to pound and squeeze
And clarify,—refine to proof
　　The liquor filtered by degrees,
While the world stands aloof.

And there's the extract, flasked and fine,
　　And priced and salable at last!
And Hobbs, Nobbs, Stokes and Nokes combine
　　To paint the future from the past,
Put blue into their line.

Hobbs hints blue,—straight he turtle eats:
  Nobbs prints blue,—claret crowns his cup:
Nokes outdares Stokes in azure feats,—
  Both gorge. Who fished the murex up?
What porridge had John Keats?

                                   —*Robert Browning*

From "Works of Cowper." To the Rev. John Newton.

MY DEAR FRIEND: I found your account of what you
experienced in your state of maiden authorship very entertaining, because very natural. I suppose that no man
ever made his first sally from the press without a conviction
that all eyes and ears would be engaged to attend him, at
least, without a thousand anxieties lest they should not.
But, however arduous and interesting such an enterprise
may be in the first instance, it seems to me that our feelings
on the occasion soon become obtuse. I can answer at least
for one. Mine are by no means what they were when
I published my first volume. I am even so indifferent to
the matter, that I can truly assert myself guiltless of the
very idea of my book, sometimes whole days together. God
knows that, my mind having been occupied more than
twelve years in the contemplation of the most distressing
subjects, the world, and its opinion of what I write, is
become as unimportant to me as the whistling of a bird in
a bush. Despair made amusement necessary, and I found
poetry the most agreeable amusement. Had I not endeavoured to perform my best, it would not have amused
me at all. The mere blotting of so much paper would have
been but indifferent sport. God gave me grace also to

wish that I might not write in vain. Accordingly I have mingled much truth with much trifle; and such truths as deserved at least to be clad as well and as handsomely as I could clothe them. If the world approve me not, so much the worse for them, but not for me. I have only endeavoured to serve them, and the loss will be their own. And as to their commendations, if I should chance to win them, I feel myself equally invulnerable there. The view that I have had of myself, for many years, has been so truly humiliating, that I think the praises of all mankind could not hurt me. God knows that I speak my present sense of the matter at least most truly, when I say that the admiration of creatures like myself seems to me a weapon the least dangerous that my worst enemy could employ against me. I am fortified against it by such solidity of real self-abasement, that I deceive myself most egregiously if I do not heartily despise it. Praise belongeth to God; and I seem to myself to covet it no more than I covet divine honours. Could I assuredly hope that God would at last deliver me, I should have reason to thank him for all that I have suffered, were it only for the sake of this single fruit of my affliction—that it has taught me how much more contemptible I am in myself than I ever before suspected and has reduced my former share of self-knowledge (of which at that time I had a tolerably good opinion) to a mere nullity, in comparison with what I have acquired since. Self is a subject of inscrutable misery and mischief, and can never be studied to so much advantage as in the dark; for as the bright beams of the sun seem to impart a beauty to the foulest objects, and can make even a dunghill smile, so the light of

God's countenance, vouchsafed to a fallen creature, so sweetens him and softens him for the time, that he seems both to others and to himself, to have nothing savage or sordid about him. *But the heart is a nest of serpents, and will be such whilst it continues to beat. If God cover the mouth of that nest with his hand, they are hush and snug; but if he withdraw his hand, the whole family lift up their heads and hiss, and are as active and venomous as ever.* This I always professed to believe from the time that I had embraced the truth, but never knew it as I know it now. To what end I have been made to know it as I do, whether for the benefit of others, or for my own, or for both, or for neither, will appear hereafter.

—William Cowper

From "Table Talk."

A. At Westminster, where little poets strive
To set a distich upon six and five,
Where Discipline helps opening buds of sense
And makes his pupils proud with silver pence,
I was a poet too; but modern taste
Is so refined, and delicate and chaste,
That verse, whatever fire the fancy warms,
Without a creamy smoothness has no charms
Thus all success depending on an ear,
And thinking I might purchase it too dear,
If sentiment were sacrified to sound,
And truth cut short to make a period round,
I judged a man of sense could scarce do worse
Than caper in the morris-dance of verse.

B. Thus reputation is a spur to wit
And some wits flag through fear of losing it.
Give me the line that ploughs its stately course,
Like a proud swan, conquering the stream by force;
That, like some cottage beauty, strikes the heart,
Quite unindebted to the tricks of art.

—William Cowper

From "Letters of Samuel Taylor Coleridge." To Thomas Allsop.

MY DEAR SIR: I cannot express how kind I felt your letter. Would to heaven I had many with feelings like yours, "accustomed to express themselves warmly and (as far as the word is applicable to you, even) enthusiastically." But, alas! during the prime manhood of my intellect I had nothing but cold water thrown on my efforts. I speak not now of my systematic and most unprovoked maligners. On *them* I have retorted only by pity and by prayer. These may have, and doubtless *have,* joined with the frivolity of "the reading public" in checking and almost in preventing the sale of my works; and so far have done injury to my *purse.* *Me* they have not injured. But I have loved with enthusiastic self-oblivion those who have been so well pleased that I should, year after year, flow with a hundred nameless rills into *their* main stream, that they could find nothing but cold praise and effective discouragement of every attempt of mine to roll onward in a distinct current of my own; who *admitted* that the "Ancient Mariner," the "Christabel," the "Remorse," and some pages of "The Friend" were not without merit, but were abundantly anxious to acquit their judgments of any blindness to the very numerous defects. Yet they *knew* that *to praise,* as mere praise, I was characteristically, almost constitutionally, indifferent. In sympathy alone I found at once nourishment and stimulus; and for sympathy *alone* did my heart crave. . . .

—Samuel Taylor Coleridge

From "Letters of Samuel Taylor Coleridge." To Thomas Poole.

. . . No grocer's apprentice, after his first month's permitted riot, was ever sicker of figs and raisins than I of hearing about the "Remorse." The endless rat-a-tat-tat at our black-and-blue-bruised door, and my three master-fiends, proof sheets, letters (for I have a raging epistolophobia), and worse than these—invitations to large dinners, which I cannot refuse without offence and imputation of pride, or accept without disturbance of temper the day before, and a sick, aching stomach for two days after, so that my spirits quite sink under it.

—Samuel Taylor Coleridge

From "Letters and Journals of Byron." To Murray.

I once wrote from the fullness of my mind and the love of fame (not as an *end,* but as a *means,* to obtain that influence over men's minds which is power in itself and in its consequences), and now from habit and from avarice; so that the effect may probably be as different as the inspiration. I have the same facility, and indeed necessity, of composition, to avoid idleness (though idleness in a hot country is a pleasure), but a much greater indifference to what is to become of it, after it has served my immediate purpose. . . .

—*Lord Byron*

From "Letters and Journals of Byron."

Crosby, my London publisher, has disposed of his second importation, and has sent to Ridge for a *third*—at least so he says. In every bookseller's window I see my *own name* and *say nothing*, but enjoy my fame in secret. My last reviewer kindly requests me to alter my determination of writing no more, and "a Friend to the Cause of Literature" begs I will *gratify* the *public* with some new work "at no very distant period." Who would not be a bard?—that is to say, if all critics would be so polite. However, the others will pay me off, I doubt not, for this *gentle* encouragement. If so, have at 'em! By-the-by, I have written at my intervals of leisure, after two in the morning, three hundred and eighty lines in blank verse, of Bosworth Field. I have luckily got Hutton's account. I shall extend the Poem to eight or ten books, and shall have finished it in a year. Whether it will be published or not must depend on circumstances. So much for *egotism!* My *laurels* have turned my brain, but the *cooling acids* of forthcoming criticisms will probably restore me to modesty.

—*Lord Byron*

From "Letters and Journals of Byron."

. . . I have now a review before me, entitled "Literary Recreations," where my *bardship* is applauded far beyond my deserts. I know nothing of the critic, but think *him* a very discerning gentleman, and *myself* a devilish *clever* fellow. His critique pleases me particularly because it is of great length, and a proper quantum of censure is administered, just to give an agreeable *relish* to the praise. You know I hate insipid, unqualified, commonplace compliment. If you wish to see it, order the 13th number of "Literary Recreations" for the last month. I assure you I have not the most distant idea of the writer of the article—it is printed in a periodical publication—and though I have written a paper (a review of Wordsworth), which appears in the same work, I am ignorant of every other person concerned in it—even the editor, whose name I have not heard. My cousin, Lord Alexander Gordon, who resided in the same hotel, told me his mother, her Grace of Gordon, requested he would introduce my *poetical* Lordship to her *Highness*, as she had bought my volume, admired it exceedingly in common with the rest of the fashionable world, and wished to claim her relationship with the author. I was unluckily engaged on an excursion for some days afterward, and as the duchess was on the eve of departure for Scotland, I have postponed my introduction till the winter, when I shall favour the lady, *whose taste I shall not dispute,* with my most sublime and edifying conversation. She is now in the Highlands, and Alexander took his departure a few days ago, for the same *blessed* seat of *"dark rolling winds."*

—*Lord Byron*

From "Pope's Works." To Bolingbroke.

. . . To write well, lastingly well, immortally well, must not one leave father and mother and cleave unto the muse? Must not one be prepared to endure the reproaches of men, want, and much fasting, nay martyrdom in its cause? It is such a task as scarcely leaves a man time to be a good neighbor, an useful friend, nay to plant a tree, much less to save his soul. . . .

—Alexander Pope

From "Life, Letters and Literary Remains of John Keats." To Haydon.

. . . There is no greater sin, after the seven deadly, than to flatter one's self into the idea of being a great poet, or one of those beings who are privileged to wear out their lives in the pursuit of honour. How comfortable a thing it is to feel that such a crime must bring its heavy penalty, that if one be a self-deluder, accounts must be balanced! I am glad you are hard at work; it will now soon be done. I long to see Wordsworth's, as well as to have mine in; but I would rather not show my face in town till the end of the year, if that would be time enough; if not I shall be disappointed if you do not write me ever when you think best. I never quite despair, and I read Shakespeare,— indeed, I shall, I think, never read any other book much; now this might lead me into a very long confab, but I desist. I am very near agreeing with Hazlitt, that Shakespeare is enough for us.

—John Keats

From "Life, Letters and Literary Remains of John Keats."
To Reynolds.

I have not the slightest feeling of humility towards the
public, or to any thing in existence but the Eternal Being,
the Principle of Beauty, and the Memory of Great Men.
When I am writing for myself, for the mere sake of the
moment's enjoyment, perhaps nature has its course with
me; but a Preface is written to the public—a thing I
cannot help looking upon as an enemy, and which I cannot
address without feelings of hostility. If I write a Preface
in a supple or subdued style, it will not be in character
with me as a public speaker.

I would be subdued before my friends, and thank them
for subduing me; but among multitudes of men I have
no feel of stooping; I hate the idea of humility to them.

—John Keats

From "Life, Letters and Literary Remains of John Keats."
To Taylor.

I feel every confidence that, if I choose, I may be a
popular writer. That I will never be; but for all that I
will get a livelihood. I equally dislike the favour of the
public with the love of a woman. They are both a cloying
treacle to the wings of independence. I shall now consider
them (the people) as debtors to me for verses, not myself
to them for admiration, which I can do without. I have
of late been indulging my spleen by composing a preface
at them; after all resolving never to write a preface at
all. *"There* are so many verses," would I have said to
them; "give so much means for me to buy pleasure with,

as a relief to my hours of labour.'' You will observe at the end of this, if you put down the letter, "How a solitary life engenders pride and egotism!'' True—I know it does: but this pride and egotism will enable me to write finer things than any thing else could, so I will indulge it. Just so much as I am humbled by the genius above my grasp, am I exalted and look with hate and contempt upon the literary world.

—*John Keats*

From "Life, Letters and Literary Remains of John Keats." Letter to George Keats.

As to what you say about my being a Poet, I can return no answer but by saying that the high idea I have of poetical fame makes me think I see it towering too high above me. At any rate I have no right to talk until "Endymion" is finished. It will be a test, a trial of my powers of imagination, and chiefly of my invention—which is a rare thing indeed—by which I must make 4000 lines of one bare circumstance, and fill them with poetry. And when I consider that this is a great task, and that when done it will take me but a dozen paces towards the Temple of Fame—it makes me say—'God forbid that I should be without such a task!' I have heard Hunt say, and (I) may be asked, *"Why endeavour after a long poem?"* To which I should answer, "Do not the lovers of poetry like to have a little region to wander in, where they may pick and choose, and in which the images are so numerous that many are forgotten and found new in a second reading—which may be food for a week's stroll in the summer?" Do they not like this better than what they can read through before Mrs. Williams comes downstairs?—a morning's work at most.

Besides a long poem is a test of invention, which I take to be the polar star of poetry, as Fancy is the sails, and Imagination the rudder. Did our great poets ever write short pieces? I mean in the shape of Tales. This same invention seems indeed of late years to have been forgotten in a partial excellence. But enough of this—I put on no laurels till I shall have finished "Endymion," and I hope Apollo is not enraged at my having made mockery of him at Hunt's.

—John Keats

From "Letters of Percy Bysshe Shelley," to Charles Ollier.

. . . The "Adonais," in spite of its mysticism, is the least imperfect of my compositions, and, as the image of my regret and honour for poor Keats, I wish it to be so. . . .

—Percy Bysshe Shelley

From "Letters of Percy Bysshe Shelley." To Joseph Severn, concerning "Adonais."

. . . In spite of his transcendent genius, Keats never was, nor ever will be, a popular poet; and the total neglect and obscurity in which the astonishing remnants of his mind still lie, was hardly to be dissipated by a writer, who, however he may differ from Keats in more important qualities, at least resembles him in that accidental one, a want of popularity.

I have little hope, therefore, that the poem I send you will excite any attention, nor do I feel assured that a critical notice of his writings would find a single reader. . . .

—*Percy Bysshe Shelley*

LINES TO A REVIEWER

Alas, good friend, what profit can you see
In hating such a hateless thing as me?
There is no sport in hate where all the rage
Is on one side: in vain would you assuage
Your frowns upon an unresisting smile,
In which not even contempt lurks to beguile
Your heart, by some faint sympathy of hate.
Oh, conquer what you cannot satiate!
For to your passion I am far more coy
Than ever yet was coldest maid or boy
In winter noon. Of your antipathy
If I am the Narcissus, you are free
To pine into a sound with hating me.

—*Percy Bysshe Shelley*

Published by Leigh Hunt, "The Literary Pocket-Book," 1823. These lines, and the "Sonnet" immediately preceding, are signed Σ in the "Literary Pocket-Book."

From "Letters of Percy Bysshe Shelley." To Charles and James Ollier.

"Prometheus Unbound," I must tell you, is my favourite poem: I charge you, therefore, specially to pet him and feed him with fine ink and good paper. "Cenci" is written for the multitude, and ought to sell well. I think, if

I may judge by its merits, the "Prometheus" cannot sell beyond twenty copies. I hear nothing either from Hunt, or you, or any one. If you condescend to write to me, mention something about Keats. . . .

If any of the Reviews abuse me, cut them out and send them. If they praise, you need not trouble yourself. I feel ashamed, if I could believe that I should deserve the latter; the former, I flatter myself, is no more than a just tribute. . . .

Percy Bysshe Shelley

From "Letters of Percy Bysshe Shelley." To John and Maria Gisborne.

I am fully repaid for the painful emotions from which some verses of my poem sprang, by your sympathy and approbation—which is all the reward I expect—and as much as I desire. It is not for me to judge whether, in the high praise your feelings assign me, you are right or wrong. The poet and the man are two different natures; though they exist together, they may be unconscious of each other, and incapable of deciding on each other's powers and efforts by any reflex act. The decision of the cause, whether or no *I* am a poet, is removed from the present time to the hour when our posterity shall assemble; but the court is a very severe one, and I fear that the verdict will be "Guilty—death!" . . .

—Percy Bysshe Shelley

POEMS WRITTEN IN 1819

AN EXHORTATION

Chameleons feed on light and air:
  Poets' food is love and fame:
If in this wide world of care
  Poets could but find the same
With as little toil as they,
    Would they ever change their hue
    As the light chameleons do,
Suiting it to every ray
  Twenty times a day?

Poets are on this cold earth,
  As chameleons might be,
Hidden from their early birth
  In a cave beneath the sea;
Where light is, chameleons change:
  Where love is not, poets do:
  Fame is love disguised: if few
Find either, never think it strange
  That poets range.

Yet dare not stain with wealth or power
  A poet's free and heavenly mind:
If bright chameleons should devour
  Any food but beams and wind,
They would grow as earthly soon
  As their brother lizards are.
  Children of a sunnier star,
Spirits from beyond the moon,
  Oh, refuse the boon!

                —Percy Bysshe Shelley

From "Introduction to the Works of Milton." To Diodati.

. . . What besides God has resolved concerning me I know not, but this at least: *He has instilled into me, if into any one, a vehement love of the beautiful.* Not with so much labour, as the fables have it, is Ceres said to have sought her daughter Proserpina as it is my habit day and night to seek for this *idea of the beautiful,* as for a certain image of supreme beauty, through all the forms and faces of things (*for many are the shapes of things divine*), and to follow it as it leads me on by some sure traces which I seem to recognize. Hence it is that, when any one scorns what the vulgar opine in their depraved estimation of things, and dares to feel and speak and be that which the highest wisdom throughout all ages has taught to be best, to that man I attach myself forthwith by a kind of real necessity, wherever I find him. If, whether by nature or by my fate, I am so circumstanced that by no effort or labour of mine can I myself rise to such an honour and elevation, yet that I should always worship and look up to those who have attained that glory, or happily aspire to it, neither gods nor men, I reckon, have bidden nay.

But now I know you wish to have your curiosity satisfied. You make many anxious inquiries, even as to what I am at present thinking of. Hearken, Theodotus, but let it be in your private ear, lest I blush; and allow me for a little to use big language with you. You ask what I am thinking of? So may the good Deity help me, of immortality! And what am I doing? *Growing my wings* and meditating flight; but as yet our Pegasus raises himself on very tender pinions. Let us be lowly wise!

—*John Milton*

POETS AND CRITICS

This thing, that thing is the rage,
Helter-skelter runs the age;
Minds on this round earth of ours
Vary like the leaves and flowers,
    Fashion'd after certain laws;
Sing thou low or loud or sweet,
All at all points thou canst not meet,
    Some will pass and some will pause.

What is true at last will tell:
Few at first will place thee well;
Some too low would have thee shine,
Some too high—no fault of thine—
    Hold thine own, and work thy will!
Year will graze the heel of year,
But seldom comes the poet here,
    And the Critic's rarer still.

—Alfred Tennyson

LITERARY SQUABBLES

Ah God! the petty fools of rhyme
    That shriek and sweat in pigmy wars
Before the stony face of Time,
    And look'd at by the silent stars:

Who hate each other for a song,
    And do their little best to bite
And pinch their brethren in the throng,
    And scratch the very dead for spite:

And strain to make an inch of room
  For their sweet selves, and cannot hear
The sullen Lethe rolling doom
  On them and theirs and all things here:

When one small touch of Charity
  Could lift them nearer God-like state
Than if the crowded Orb should cry
  Like those who cried Diana great:

And I too, talk, and lose the touch
  I talk of. Surely, after all,
The noblest answer unto such
  Is perfect stillness when they brawl.

—Alfred Tennyson

From "The Letters of Algernon Charles Swinburne." To Lady Trevelyan.

As to my poems, my perplexity is this: that no two friends have ever given me the same advice. Now more than ever I would rather take yours than another's; but I see neither where to begin nor when to stop. I have written nothing to be ashamed of. I have been advised to suppress *Atalanta,* to cancel *Chastelard,* and so on till not a line of my work would have been left. Two days ago Ruskin called on me and stayed for a long evening, during which he heard a great part of my forthcoming volume of poems, selected with a view to secure his advice as to publication and the verdict of the world of readers and writers. It was impossible to have a fairer judge. I have not known him long or intimately; and he is neither a rival nor a reviewer. I can only say that I was sincerely surprised by the enjoyment he seemed to derive from my work, and the frankness with which he accepted it. Any poem which all my friends for whose opinion I care had advised me to omit, should be omitted. But I never have written such an one. Some for example which you have told me were favourites of yours, such as the *Hymn to Proserpine* of the "Last Pagan"—I have been advised to omit as likely to hurt the feeling of a religious public. I cannot but see that whatever I do will be assailed and misconstrued by those who can do nothing and who detest their betters.

—Algernon Charles Swinburne

From "The Letters of Algernon Charles Swinburne." To Lord Houghton.

. . . In answer to something that Mr. Landor said today of his own age, I reminded him of his equals and predecessors, Sophocles and Titian; he said he should not live up to the age of Sophocles—not see ninety. I don't see why he shouldn't, if he has people about him to care for him as he should be cared for. I should like to throw up all other things on earth and devote myself to playing valet to him for the rest of his days. I would black his boots if he were *chez moi*. He has given me the shock of adoration which one feels at thirteen towards great men. I am not sure that any other emotion is so endurable and persistently delicious as that of worship, when your god is indubitable and incarnate before your eyes.

—Algernon Charles Swinburne

From "Letters." To Mrs. Forster.

Many thanks, my dearest K., for your extracts. My poems are making their way, I think, though slowly, and perhaps never to make way very far. There must always be some people, however, to whom the literalness and sincerity of them has a charm. After all, that American review, which hit upon this last—their sincerity—as their most interesting quality, was not far wrong. It seems to me strange, sometimes to hear of people taking pleasure in this or that poem which was written years ago, which then nobody took pleasure in but you, which I then perhaps wondered that nobody took pleasure in, but since had made up my mind that nobody was likely to. The fact is, however, that the state of mind expressed in many of the poems is one that is becoming more common, and you see that even the Obermann stanzas are taken up with interest by some.

—Matthew Arnold

That critic must indeed be bold
Who pits new authors against old.
Only the ancient coin is prized,
The dead alone are canonized:
What was even Shakespeare until then?
A poet scarce compared with Ben:
And Milton in the streets no taller
Than sparkling easy-ambling Waller.
Waller now walks with riming crowds,
While Milton sits above the clouds,

Above the stars, his fix'd abode,
And points to men their way to God.

—*Walter Savage Landor*

From "The Letters of William Blake." To Flaxman.

And now begins a new life, because another covering of
earth is shaken off. I am more famed in Heaven for my
works than I could well conceive. In my brain are studies
and chambers filled with books and pictures of old, which
I wrote and painted in ages of eternity before my mortal
life; and those works are the delight and study of archangels. Why, then, should I be anxious about the riches
or fame of mortality? The Lord our Father will do for
us and with us according to His divine will for our good.

—*William Blake*

PRIDE ALLOWABLE IN POETS

As thou deserv'st be proud; then gladly let
The Muse give thee the Delphic coronet.

—*Robert Herrick*

GLORY

I make no haste to have my numbers read;
Seldom comes glory till a man be dead.

—*Robert Herrick*

POETRY PERPETUATES THE POET

Here I myself might likewise die,
And utterly forgotten lie,
But that eternal poetry,
Repullulation gives me here,
Until the thirtieth thousand year,
When all the dead shall reappear.

—*Robert Herrick*

Come, said my soul,
Such verses for my body let us write, (for we are one,)
That should I after death invisibly return,
Or, long, long hence, in other spheres,
There to some group of mates the chants resuming,
(Tallying earth's soil, trees, winds, tumultuous waves,)
Ever with pleas'd smile I may keep on,
Ever and ever yet the verses owning—as, first, I here and
  now,
Signing for soul and body, set to them my name.

—*Walt Whitman*

INDEX OF AUTHORS

The author of this book has quoted only British and American authors. The other authorities named in this index are mentioned in the passages quoted.

LIST OF WORKS QUOTED